THE MASQUE OF KINGS

THE MASQUE OF KINGS

KINGS

A PLAY IN THREE ACTS

BY
MAXWELL ANDERSON

ANDERSON HOUSE
NEW YORK · WASHINGTON

MDCCCCXXXVII

NOTE

COMPOSED, PRINTED, AND BOUND BY GEORGE BANTA PUBLISHING
COMPANY, MENASHA, WISCONSIN

For Mab

PREFACE

To the Reader—

This play, having stood its trial in the theatre, and having emerged therefrom, not scathless but with some golden opinions, it is now offered in the usual fashion to those who for any reason wish to read what has been set down for the stage; but with this difference, that the whole play is here offered as it came first from the author's hand, all its members intact, head, arms, legs, private parts and other flourishes, and without record of the chipping, chopping, haggling, hacking and disemboweling which is insisted on by most producers on Broadway and which may make a play shorter, or longer, or more effective in the theatre, but will always subtract from its quality.

M. A.

CHARACTERS

IN ORDER OF APPEARANCE:

Franz Joseph

Koinoff

A Servant

Elizabeth

Taafe

Baronin von Neustadt

Baron von Neustadt

Loschek

1st Lady

1st Man

2nd Lady

2nd Man

3rd Man

Rudolph

Bratfisch

A Girl

Mary Vetsera

Archduke John

Sceps

Rauscher

Hoyos

THE MASQUE OF KINGS

ACT ONE

ACT I

SCENE 1

SCENE: *A corner of the study of the Emperor Franz Joseph in the Hofburg, Vienna. It is late at night in January, 1889, but the emperor is still at work, standing before a high desk covered with letters and papers. Tapers burn over the desk. There is no other light. Behind the emperor are a table and a chair, the table also covered with papers.* CAPTAIN KOINOFF *stands near the table.*

Franz Joseph. Proceed, proceed, man. I can hear you while I work.

Koinoff. Yes, Your Majesty.

Franz Joseph. Or shall I tell you what you were about to say? [*He slits an envelope.*]

A well-known oratorical bastard named the Archduke John of Tuscany—so far right?—

Koinoff. Yes, Majesty.

Franz Joseph. Will confer tonight with the Archduke Rudolph. In his company will be—let me think—a well-known radical editor named Sceps, a soft-brained family man with a profound conviction that the whole world can be set right by the simple expedient of turning everything upside down, including, I surmise, the imperial navy, the city reservoir and his own gravy boat.—The presence will also be graced by an obscure young expert in military affairs, Koinoff by name, yourself in fact, and the meeting will take place at—shall we say the residence of the Archduke John?

Koinoff. No, Majesty—the apartments of the Crown Prince Rudolph.

Franz Joseph. Dear me, in the Hofburg itself.

[*There is a knock at the door and a* SERVANT *parts the curtain.*]

You know, of course, that I am not disturbed here at this hour.

3

Servant. Yes, Your Majesty.

Franz Joseph. There is someone dead—or dying?

Servant. No, Your Majesty.

Franz Joseph. There has been a calamity in the kingdom of which
   I must be apprised instantly?

Servant. No, Your Majesty.

Franz Joseph. Then henceforth remember your orders.

Servant. Your Majesty, the Empress wishes to speak with you.

Franz Joseph. The Empress. Where is the Empress?

Servant. In the reception room, Your Majesty.
   [*A pause.*]

Franz Joseph. I will see her at once.
   [*The Servant goes.*]

   Go out through my room. I understand then that the three
   of you will take up the question of modern government?

Koinoff. That's the whole story, Your Majesty.

Franz Joseph. This way.
   [*He ushers Koinoff out. The servant ushers in the* EMPRESS *and with-
      draws.*]

   I'm more than honored.
   You see before you a workman at his labors,
   a bit dusty, I fear, and worn.

Elizabeth. You've always worked
   while others slept, dear Franz.

Franz Joseph. You wish to sit?
   I'll stand, myself. It's all my exercise—
   stooping for papers.
   [*He stoops to retrieve a fallen letter.*]

Elizabeth. Thank you.
   [*She sits.*]
    I'm afraid
I'm quite inopportune.

Franz Joseph. It's thirteen years
   as I remember it, since you've come through
   this doorway. At that time you said, if I
   recall correctly, you would not see me again,
   you would not see me any more alone
   till I answered you a question. It's not answered.
   But I should be very busy indeed, dear Cissie,
   If I'd no time to give you.

Elizabeth. Let the question go.
   And the quarrel. It's too late to rescue now
   what the flood carried with it to the sea
   so many years ago. All our deaths and loves
   go down the wash.—No it was something else
   I wanted to save now—I've passed your door
   some thousand nights, and listened, and gone by—
   it was never the moment.

Franz Joseph. Something I could grant you—
   something to ask? Among all petitioners
   you would stand first.

Elizabeth. Still?

Franz Joseph. Yes. You no longer love me,
   I know, but I love you still, and will, no doubt,
   while the pump goes. This has been our misfortune,
   yours more than mine.

Elizabeth. I've been too fortunate
   in many things. Or was when I was young.
   As we grow older and need our luck it fails.

Perhaps we take it for granted, and the gods,
the non-existent gods, are angry with us,
having spoiled us earlier.

Franz Joseph. Non-existent?

Elizabeth. There—
let's not quarrel about it—let's believe
what we believe. When you took me and made me Empress,
long ago, that was luck, unbelievable luck
for a younger daughter of the Wittelsbachs,
a footless, scandalous tribe, with nothing to offer
but my footless, scandalous ways, and a little beauty
that faded under the lamps.

Franz Joseph. It's not faded, Cissie,
and I think it never will.

Elizabeth. Well, beauty or not,
you found me out for the ne'er-do-well I was,
and I found you more emperor than mine,
and things have happened that won't be forgiven
on either side, no matter how you love
or how thick the years mulch over.

Franz Joseph. Yes. It's true.—
This what you wished to say?

Elizabeth. No. Oh, I'm clear
in my mind, Franz, though I may have given you cause
to wonder these last years. I know how strict
you guard your time, and wouldn't waste it. Here's
my business, stated plainly, quite without grief
or a woman's art. We have two things left to us
out of the wreck of years and youth: the empire,
and Rudolph, our son, who will rule it by and by,
if all goes well. I think we shall lose them both
if things go as they are.

Franz Joseph. Yes?

Elizabeth. I gave you an heir—
    my one gift to the kingdom, but a noble one;
    such a prince as an emperor, dreaming of sons,
    could wish no happier issue. Magnanimous, wise,
    beyond his years, gentle but manly, eager
    to serve, a lover of justice. This was true?

Franz Joseph. Yes.

Elizabeth. But now he's thirty years old, and this last two years
    the furies begin to tear at him. Perhaps
    my ways and yours at war in his blood. Perhaps
    inaction, and the cynicism of courts
    corrode more readily when a mind's been brought
    to a delicate perfection. A peasant brain
    resists and keeps right on. It's an evil court,
    but it doesn't touch you—nor me.

Franz Joseph. Come then—our Rudolph?

Elizabeth. I'm troubled over the news from Hungary.
    It's a freedom-loving people, never ours
    except by conquest. There's but one way to keep them—
    that's to extend the suffrage, rule them gentler
    than they can rule themselves—give without asking
    more than they think to ask.

Franz Joseph. This is like old times.

Elizabeth. It's as true now as then.

Franz Joseph. Proceed. I'll listen.

Elizabeth. Partly because he's my son, and they believe
    I've been their friend, partly because he speaks
    for all their hopes, the Hungarians have loved Rudolph,
    and he could hold them in the empire for you.

You were emperor at eighteen. It's a discipline
that Rudolph needs; power in his hands; we grow
by what we have to do. I've thought of this
a long while now. Divide your empire. Set
our Rudolph over Hungary.

Franz Joseph. As king?

Elizabeth. As king of Hungary.

Franz Joseph. I'm growing old then?

Elizabeth. No, but he'll have it in the end. You'll live
for many years, I hope.—Is he to come
to full dominion in a late middle age
when he's been burned out hollow with idleness
and lusts—all his fine faith soured to mockeries
with waiting—?

Franz Joseph. Have you spoken with Rudolph?

Elizabeth. No.

Franz Joseph. You've never told me a lie, and I believe you—
else I should think you must have spoken with him.
When have you seen our son?

Elizabeth. Why, yesterday.

Franz Joseph. To talk with him? As a mother might with a son?
I think not within the year.

Elizabeth. It may be—longer.

Franz Joseph. Then let me enlighten you concerning Rudolph.
I have a message here from His Holiness
that enlightened me this morning. Our son's petitioned
the Pope to set him free of his present marriage,
free to marry again. I have no doubt
he has in mind the same Vetsera harlot

who shares his bed at present. Even you should grant
this would make a kingly stench for the new-born court
of a new-born kingdom in Europe.

Elizabeth. Yes.

Franz Joseph. That's first.
Second, the state of Hungary's aflame,
of late, and I think our Rudolph set the fire—
with plots to make him king, blow me aside
like the old dodderer over desks I am,
oh, leave me Austria if I care to keep it,
but Hungary for Rudolph, Rudolph for Hungary,
caps in the air, the old men in their places—
somewhat to the rear, or slightly underground
if they're in the way—a young man on the throne,
and let the bugles blow! You knew of this?

Elizabeth. No.

Franz Joseph. Well, I've known—perhaps as much as any,
and more than they know I know. If you'd be kind
to Rudolph, tell him this; that his hot friends
would better cool their heads or they'll cool their heels;
they're too hot by half.

Elizabeth. Rudolph began this?

Franz Joseph. I don't know. I can't swear it. It seems likely,
judging by what he's written, by the friends he hugs
and the rendezvous he keeps. But to be just
I don't know how far it's his.

Elizabeth. If it were so
that Hungary does wish it—wish him for king—
you would oppose it still?

Franz Joseph. A state will wish
what it's told to wish. It has no will of its own.

Elizabeth. But what I've asked—could so easily be done—
　　without loss, even with gain to you. When we
　　were young together, you lightened your hand one day
　　over Hungary for my sake—and in time,
　　for I think it won them—

Franz Joseph. I should oppose it still.
　　Not that it's treason to me—all these things
　　are words—faith, treason, honor—behind them lie
　　realities of government which I face
　　daily here at my desk. No—let me go back.
　　When I first saw you you were not seventeen,
　　and beautiful in some sad crystal fashion
　　that's quite beyond the phrasing of an old man
　　who's made himself book-keeper to an empire
　　and sloughed the graces. If I told you then
　　I came too short in the telling—by some worlds
　　I came too short. I loved you instantly,
　　beyond recking costs, must have you; we were married,
　　the year went by like summer lightning, then
　　I looked behind the laughter on your face
　　and found an anarch, a laughing devil, stronger
　　than I was, quicker of wit, a child in purpose,
　　a demon in desire. You never once
　　put out your hand but to tear down the kingdom,
　　riddle authority, and with that seraph's face
　　and seraph's tongue seduced me to betrayals
　　that bind me yet. And still I loved you, still
　　I could not tear you out, and Rudolph came,
　　his mother's child, an archangel's face and tongue
　　again, with a devil's will, a Wittelsbach
　　as they've been from the beginning. But I loved him—
　　as I loved you—almost as I loved you.
　　He hates me and betrays me—and I love him.
　　All my life long I tread my own heart down

here in the dust and silence of this room
where no one enters. I shall defend my kingdom
and hold it, and send it on despite you, yes,
despite my love for you and him. Go now.
I have work to do.

Elizabeth. I shall not ask again.

Franz Joseph. I have been patient with Rudolph, and shall be
  patient.
  He may be a son to me yet—but as for you
  when you loved elsewhere, when you took your body,
  the body of the Empress, and laid it down
  beside another man, and took him to you—
  when I heard this I heard my own death walking
  the palace hallways, stepping off my days
  and no other step to wait for.

Elizabeth. You were the first
  in that, remember.

Franz Joseph. A man may be unfaithful,
  but not a woman, and not an empress.

Elizabeth. No?
  Well, that has been changed, I think.

Franz Joseph. It has not been changed.

Elizabeth. You've chewed on your revenge these many years.
  Surely it's been enough, Franz. Where is Imry?

Franz Joseph. Where you'll not see him,
  where you would hardly care to see him now,
  no place for lovers.
    [*She steps back.*]

Elizabeth. Goodnight.

Franz Joseph. Goodnight.

Elizabeth. This step
    you hear in the halls, it may not be your death
    but only a girl you loved one time, grown old
    and sleepless, hurrying now a little toward
    a too-long corridor's end. You're of tougher grain
    than I—or Rudolph. You'll outlive us; when
    you bury us the halls will be quieter.
> [*She goes out through the curtain. Franz Joseph takes up the paper-weight on his desk, as if to resume his work, puts it down and sits, his eyes on the floor.* COUNT TAAFE *enters.*]

Taafe. Your Majesty.

Franz Joseph. Yes? Yes, Taafe.

Taafe. You asked me to come in without announcement
    when it was certain the Vetsera girl
    had come alone to Rudolph.

Franz Joseph. She's with him?

Taafe. Yes.

Franz Joseph. We must be sure.

Taafe. There's a serving maid who watches
    about Prince Rudolph's door. I'll wager on it;
    so far she's made no errors.

Franz Joseph. Then we'll go.
> [*He takes a step, then puts out his hand to the table.*]

One moment.

Taafe. Your Majesty's not well?

Franz Joseph. It's nothing.
> [*He sits*]

Nothing, I shall wish you to come with me.
They'll be alone together?

Taafe. For a time.
   However, I have also information
   the Archduke John may visit him tonight,
   and it seems reliable.

Franz Joseph. The Archduke John.

Taafe. That's the Hungarian business.
   I should have thought the woman was enough,
   but when we're young we take it in our stride,
   amours and intrigue after midnight.—Sleep?
   Sleep later on, while the alarm rings. Still,
   we may find it awkward.

Franz Joseph. Say nothing of Hungary.
   One thing at a time, and the woman first.

Taafe. Very well.

Franz Joseph. What do you think of Rudolph, Taafe, frankly,
   forgetting I'm his father?

Taafe. Frankly, sire,
   he's a rebel and a rake.

Franz Joseph. I'd give these arms
   here at the shoulder, I'd step down in a grave
   tonight, let them stop my mouth and ears with earth
   to have another son. It may be I
   won't live forever. God send me the wit I need
   to save my empire from the son I have.
   I'm better. We can go.
     [*They go out.*]

CURTAIN

ACT I

SCENE 2

SCENE: *A room—half living-room and half study, in the apartments of the Crown Prince Rudolph of Austria, at the Hofburg. A door to the right leads to a reception-chamber, a door at the rear to the interior of the apartment and the bedroom. To the right rear a desk stands under a shelf of books, a skull grinning among the writing materials. At the left rear a fire burns in the fireplace. In the left wall are high French windows. Over the desk hangs a portrait of Rudolph's mother, the Empress Elizabeth, as a young girl, her hair crowned with stars. It is after midnight, the room ablaze with light.*

THREE MEN *and* THREE WOMEN, *dressed for a masked ball, lounge and stand about the room, as if waiting. Among them are the* BARON *and* BARONIN VON NEUSTADT. *A domino lies across the couch, ready to be donned.*

Baronin von Neustadt. Your question, then, sir. Your question. I am ready for your question.

[*She seats herself before one of the men.*]

Baron von Neustadt. My dear, where were you yesterday afternoon?

The Baronin. At home, my love. Proceed.

von Neustadt. Be more specific. Where, definitely where?

The Baronin. In my own bedroom, heart's darling.

von Neustadt. Ah, and your occupation?

The Baronin. I was burning—old letters.

1st Lady. Yes, that's true, she told me. She was burning old letters.

1st Man. All afternoon?

The Baronin. My dear Fritzi, all afternoon.

1st Man. A bale of letters.

The Baronin. Oh, quite a bale. At least.

14

von Neustadt. Ah—ah!—Then how did it happen, my only love—
I call you to witness, d'Orsay—how did it happen that Mimi
waited for you all afternoon in your bedroom, and saw nothing
of you—no wraith of you, no glimpse, from two till six—

1st Man. What, saw no flame, smelled no smoke, no burning?

von Neustadt. There was nobody there—!

The Baronin. The slut lies.

2nd Lady. Oh, no, darling. I tell the truth.

von Neustadt. Rudi—Rudi!

The Baronin. He's about to complain to royalty.

von Neustadt. By God, I shall buy a whip! Rudi! Rudi!

Loschek.
    [*Entering from the bedroom*]
  The prince will be with you in a moment, sir.

The Baronin. And now will you answer my questions, sweetest
of the sweet?

von Neustadt. No.

The Baronin. Come, I give you the witness chair. And to begin,
where were you, my lord and master, yesterday afternoon?

2nd Man. In church. He told me.

3rd. Man. In medias res.
    [RUDOLPH *enters in a dressing gown.*]

Rudolph. Why the outcry?

von Neustadt. Rudi! She refuses to tell me where she was!

Rudolph. She? Who, dear baron?

von Neustadt. That one there! My wife there!

Rudolph. Must you take up our time with these domestic details?

von Neustadt. But it's incessant! No matter where I expect her to be she's always somewhere else!

Rudolph. But how fortunate you are in your family arrangements, and how some men would envy you!

von Neustadt. You think so?

The Baronin. My love, you exaggerate!

von Neustadt. Not at all.

2nd Man. You are coming with us, Your Highness?

Rudolph. I meant to, but some servant of the state has left a pile of documents on my desk—you see?

1st Man. They must be signed?

Rudolph. They must be signed—tonight.

1st Lady. And you must read them?

Rudolph. I must read them.

1st Lady.
   Shall we do him the honor of believing him?
1st Man.
   [*Looking up at the portrait of the Empress*]
   I swear there's never in the history of the world been a woman as beautiful as the Empress.

2nd Lady. Isn't it true? And she's still beautiful.

2nd Man. God knows where Rudi got his looks.

The Baronin. There was a certain master of horse much favored of the Empress about our Rudolph's time. An oaf, but ingratiating. Methinks a resemblance has been traced—

Rudolph. Trail your slime where else you will, you rout of bitchery, but keep your tongues now and forever from my mother! [*A pause.*]

1st Lady. Come, come, darling, you attack the succession.

The Baronin. Yes,—I'm sorry. After all, a prince's mother is sacred. Will you forgive my offending?

Rudolph. Some other time, shall we say? Tonight I find you not so much offending as offensive.

The Baronin. You will make enemies.

Rudolph. I have made them—many and terrible.

The Baronin. Do you wish to add me to the list?

Rudolph. There was once a grandam, you may remember, who added water to the sea?

The Baronin. I do remember.

Rudolph. Ponder it.

The Baronin. I would much rather be friends with you, Your Highness. And you'll need friends. You are playing a deep and devious game in the Hungarian elections. You are involved far beyond safety with the Baroness Vetsera. You have offended your father on both these counts, and there is a limit to the tolerance even of an emperor.

von Neustadt. For God's sake, darling!

Rudolph. Not because you are dangerous, but for your honesty, I will be friends with you, my dear Baronin, and I will admit that the court of Vienna is a high and slippery place, whence a breath, a reaching out, may send one down the escarpments to oblivion. But for myself I have leaped, I have slid, I have positively dived over the parapets, only to find myself replaced with miraculous celerity upon the topmost point of this distasteful pinnacle, I loathe the court of Vienna, I despise the people who inhabit it, I despise myself for making a part of it, yet here I am and have been, any time this thirty years. What you say of my relations to Hungary and to the Baroness Vetsera, these are lies, rumor, scandal, what you like, but repeat them infinitely, I beg of you—give me what push you can from this glassy eminence, and you will be a friend indeed.

The Baronin. But you're in earnest, your Highness.

Rudolph. Is that a capital crime in your circle?

The Baronin. It always makes me a little uncomfortable.

Rudolph. Oh! that's beyond pardon!

The Baronin. But do you actually despise the court of Vienna?

Rudolph. And loathe it.

The Baronin. Then I'm saved from boredom for another fortnight. I too shall despise the court of Vienna. I shall wither it with scorn, I shall drench it with adjectives. Children, we shall make this the latest thing. The Habsburg court! Its incredible morals! Its perfervid asininities! Despise it? I loathe it! It's— putrid!—Rudi! Rudi! We shall make you the height of fashion!

Rudolph. Be off with you, all of you. You're late, and so am I.

The Baronin. Nevertheless I'm more your friend than you guess. I have had the confidence of a certain person, but hush, we say nothing.

2nd Lady. Are we going?

1st Man. Come, you rout of bitchery!

1st Lady. That's the word.

von Neustadt. But we'll see you, Highness?

Rudolph. In half an hour.

The Baronin. Come, refuse! Excrescences of a tawdry royalty! Come!

von Neustadt. Your word, Rudi!
> [*They go out, leaving Rudolph alone. He waits for a moment, then calls.*]

Rudolph. Loschek.

Loschek.
> [*Entering*]

Your Highness?

Rudolph. Look in the little passage, and bring Bratfisch to me.
> [*Loschek bows and returns through the inner rooms. Rudolph sits at his desk, lifts a paper from the pile and leafs through it, then thrusts it back. Loschek returns with* BRATFISCH, *and stands waiting.*]

Bratfisch. There was something, sir?

Rudolph. Yes.
> [*He draws his hand over his eyes wearily.*]

Loschek—there are too many lights.
> [*Loschek bows and begins to extinguish the candelabra, leaving two candles that burn under the portrait of the Empress.*]

What's the weather tonight?

Bratfisch. A light snow, Your Highness. It may fall an inch or two.

Rudolph. You're to wait at the postern till the lady comes, Bratfisch. Afterward Loschek will take your place. You understand?

Bratfisch. No, sir.

Rudolph. He will take your place because you will assume this domino—this—the arms here—the eyes here—

Bratfisch. Yes, sir—

Rudolph. And will be driven to the Baltazzi palace, where you will be announced as the Crown Prince Rudolph.

Bratfisch. Very well, sir.

Rudolph. Comport yourself accordingly, with grace, with dignity, above all with fitting reserve. Remain not more than a quarter of an hour. I should not suggest any passages with the ladies— beyond a discreet compliment here and there.

Bratfisch. Yes, sir.

Rudolph. Go now and take the domino with you.

Bratfisch. If you'll pardon me, Highness, there's a little man at the area-gate offering to sell chestnuts.

Rudolph. Did you make a purchase?

Bratfisch. I'm his only customer so far.

Rudolph. An agent?

Bratfisch. He's been posted there by somebody—to see who goes out and in.

Rudolph. Then he'll follow my domino. See that my domino makes a night of it, Bratfisch. A little of everything disreputable, and back here at dawn or thereabout.

Bratfisch. Yes, Highness.

> [*Bratfisch bows, takes up the domino and goes out with Loschek. Rudolph looks up at the picture of Elizabeth.*]

Rudolph. We live too long—is that what you say, my mother, with the stars in your hair? A woman outlives her beauty, a man outlives his dreams. When they painted you so, with the stars, there was brightness on your earth— dew on the lawns in spring. But now you walk

the long cold Hofburg corridors at night—
silent—and if you meet me there—your son—
you look at me as if you walked the moon
and men were strange. But then you're all courtesy:
you murmur "Rudolph, darling" and go on
and it's the moon again. We're lost and damned
here in the Hofburg. You know it; you know I'll find it—
why tell me before my time?—

[*The clock strikes twice outside.*]

   Count it out, count it,
you bells that turned back Atilla! I'm in
my thirtieth year. There's half a life left yet
before I'm cold. Would it be something gained
if I'd put roads and water enough between
my corpus and Vienna, before I die,
to evade that damned Capuchin church? It reeks
of Habsburgs and rotted kings. Must you rest there,
dear mother, when you're dead? You tell me yes—
they have plucked out the stars from your eyes and hair
and made you ready.

[*He sits, hidden in the shadow. The place is quiet for a moment, then
a* MAID *tiptoes in gently and goes to the fireplace. She busies
herself with the fire, pausing meanwhile to listen. Rudolph
moves. She rises quickly.*]

The Girl. I'm sorry—I thought—everyone was gone.

[*She starts out.*]

Rudolph. Wait.

The Girl. Yes, Your Highness. I'm sorry.

Rudolph. Who sent you here?

The Girl. No one, sir. It's—something I'm supposed to do.

Rudolph. Yes, of course.

The Girl. I may go, sir?

Rudolph. Yes.

The Girl. Thank you.

Rudolph. Wait again. Wait one moment. I know you.

The Girl. No, sir.

Rudolph. From many years ago.

The Girl. No, sir.

Rudolph. Oh, yes! I troubled your innocence, I believe,
   and gave you money, and let you go. I'm sorry.
   But why are you here?

The Girl. It—happened. I earn my living
   here in the palace.

Rudolph. Who hired you?

The Girl. The major domo.

Rudolph. And by what pretense of duty do you prowl
   my rooms after midnight?

The Girl. To see that—there's no disorder—
   and they said you were gone—

Rudolph. This is the seventh.
   One after another I uncover them,
   these household spies they set on me. And this,
   this they thought was clever—a girl I'd known,
   one with a pretty face—I might slip again,
   and you'd pick secrets between kisses—yes,
   and tattle to the Emperor.

The Girl. No, no!

Rudolph. Why not? He pays preposterously. When you're used
   and full of secrets you'll be silenced with
   a pension and well guarded! Who set you here
   and what were your instructions?

The Girl. But it's not—true—

Rudolph. You have a brain! You know what happens when
   they hang a spy on the ramparts! Tell me who's
   your master, where you give your reports, who pays
   at the end of the week, or you'll go back in a basket
   to this same major domo!

The Girl—Your Highness—

Rudolph. No lies—
   for I tell you I'm sick of this spying; they crawl in
       the walls
   like typhus-lice at plague-time! By God, I'll hang you
   in sheets from a bedpost!

The Girl. No, my lord—no, truly.
   I'm only here in the palace to earn my way—
   I've said nothing about you.

Rudolph. But I'm not wrong.

The Girl. Oh, you are. Please let me go. You've hurt my hand—
   please, will I lose my place?

Rudolph. No. I was wrong.
   Forgive me. It gets under the skin and into
   the blood, the business of being a prince. In the end
   you fancy yourself a god, and all other flesh
   an offering to you.

The Girl. I know.

Rudolph. How do you know it?

The Girl. It was so before.

Rudolph. Was it so even then,
when I was twenty-three? Perhaps it was—
I took you, and paid you off. But it grows with the years,
even though you know your flesh is grass like the rest,
even though you swear it daily, still when they bring you
food on gold, and armies tread the night
to ensure your sleep, and when you stretch out your arm
they run to make a garden—it taints the mind,
this mindless service, till what you wish you must have,
no matter how many bleed for it. I'm unjust,
and violent, and revengeful—they've made me so—
they'd make you so in my place. And so, forgive me.

The Girl. I—forgive you?

Rudolph. Yes.

The Girl. Yes, if you wish, Your Highness.

Rudolph. I say this for myself—
not for you, my dear. I've schooled myself
to live my birth down, make apology
where apologies are due, though I writhe within
to say the words. I thank you for your forgiveness.
We'll let it end there.

The Girl.
   [*Falling on her knees, taking his hand*]

My lord, let me thank you—

Rudolph. No!
Keep off your knees!
   [*Loschek enters from within.*]

Yes?

Loschek. You're not at liberty,
  Your Highness?

Rudolph. What is it? Yes.

Loschek. There's someone waiting.

Rudolph. Go now.
  [*The Girl bows and slips out.*]

Loschek. The Baroness Vetsera's here.

Rudolph. Let her in quickly.

Loschek. If I may mention it,
  we suspect this girl—this that was on her knees.

Rudolph. I know—I think you're wrong. But follow her,
  look through the hall.
  [*Loschek goes out after the Girl. Rudolph goes to the inner door.*]
  Marie!

Mary Vetsera.
  [*At the door*]
  May I come in?

Rudolph. How did you come?

Mary. Does it matter? It's snowing, sweet,
  and I walked through the snow. I wasn't followed.
  I'm sure I wasn't.

Rudolph. It doesn't matter now—
  now that I have you. Here's a whole snowflake yet
  caught in your hair. Your cheeks are cool. Good God,
  how you transform a room!

Mary. Don't you want to kiss me?

Rudolph. Does one make love with an angel, darling? Wait—
  surely one should worship a little first,

light a fire on an altar, or burn incense,
and kneel in prayer.

Mary. But not to me.

Rudolph. Yes, sweet,
to you.

Mary. Then all the gods grant all your prayers,
as suddenly.
[*She lifts her lips and he kisses her.*]
Have you been well?

Rudolph. Well enough.
I saw you once in the Prater.

Mary. I know. I saw you.
[*Loschek comes back unobtrusively through the room.*]
God in heaven, these two weeks! Oh, Rudi,
have you been lonely?

Rudolph. I've been miserable,
creeping about on trains, listening to welcomes,
fat mayors of fat towns making fat speeches
unto eternity, no word from you—

Mary. I couldn't manage. Verily, I'd have died
only for your black blessed raven Loschek
and the little note he dropped like manna in
my prayer book. Then I took up heart and lived
to see you.

Rudolph. Do you love me so much?

Mary. And more,
more than I tell you.

Rudolph. How long will it keep on?

Mary. Oh, easily till I die.—And afterward—
    I doubt that it will be much different then.

Rudolph. Oh, child, child.

Mary. Oh, truly, Rudi! I'll die
    when you die—even if you should be away
    I'd know if you were dead, and I'd die too,
    yes, where your earth was mine would find yours out
    and lie there with you.

Rudolph. Pretty.

Mary. And keep you warm—
    for there'd be such a burning in the dust
    that used to be my heart, I'd keep you warm
    deep under ground. You'll know me by the fire
    there in the dust, and then we can make up
    for never having spent a whole night together—
    lying quite still, a long while.

Rudolph. You speak too well.

Mary. Well, but I've never spoken well before,
    and never will again. It's now, for you.
    And then that's all.

Rudolph. Surely you know, dear Mary,
    this is a profitless passion for a girl
    whose family looks to her to marry the Indies
    and make her face their fortune.

Mary. Have I asked for money?

Rudolph. No. God knows I've none to give.

Mary. But then—
    my family does well enough.

Rudolph. Some time
 there will be reasons of state why I can't see you.
 My wife will rattle the gates of the Vatican,
 and bring the emperor down on us. Somehow
 they'll ship me off to the east and you to the west
 and no amount of loving will help. You'll find
 you have to wed a banker. Then your price
 will have gone down, after the scandal here,
 and I'll have spoiled your name.

Mary. If it must be,
 it must. But if I marry, still I'll love you—
 even if you go back to the Fleming—even—
 if—you should want to.

Rudolph. Would you love me then?

Mary. Yes.—This is a bitter welcome—after
 so long away.—Do you wish me to go now?

Rudolph. No.

Mary. Will it be soon?

Rudolph. I don't know.

Mary. Yes.
 I won't ask for more than I can have.
 Only—let me see you while I can.—
 It can end—when it ends.

Rudolph. May I be eaten
 of worms before my time for this! Look, sweet,
 this is a letter I wrote two weeks ago
 to the sacred nose in Rome—and here's a ring
 I've carried in my pocket this two weeks
 to give you when you came! But my damned soul
 has been so cursed and crawled upon with punks

and serving men and women I feel the itch
in every palm I touch, and taste the greed
in every kiss!

Mary. But I'm greedy, too. Too greedy.

Rudolph. Look at the letter.

Mary. What is it?

Rudolph. A petition,
drawn up formally, wherewithals and flourish,
requesting that the Pope annul my marriage
with the Princess Stephanie, on sufficient grounds,
that I may marry again.

Mary. Must you marry again?

Rudolph. This ring's to be yours.

Mary. But it's a wedding ring.

Rudolph. Perhaps if you should study it a little
and look inside the circlet you might find
a date graved. Now the dark blood climbs in your throat
remembering.

Mary. This is worse than mockery;
it's torment, Rudi. Were you free as fire
we could never marry.

Rudolph. No?

Mary. With an empire waiting?
Marry a Baltazzi out of the east,
a daughter of peddlers?

Rudolph. Why then goodbye to the empire!
They may keep it. And luck to them who get it.
It's been no luck to me.

Mary. Goodbye to the empire?—
  Now I know you mock me. I'm a girl,
  foolish, and easily gulled, but this I know—
  no prince throws up an empire for a woman
  who's been his for the asking.

Rudolph. Oh, Vienna!
  The wisdom of Vienna! All her daughters
  have eaten it with their porridge! But it's true
  that I'm no jingling poet, to sell a crown
  for love and a pair of shoes. If I wanted empire,
  I'd have the empire, and you, and Stephanie,
  and anything I whistled for! But when
  I say the Habsburg crown's an ancestral curse
  and I won't wear it, then the bars go up
  around me, and I feel my father's hand
  closing on what I do and where I go,
  till the Hofburg's a prison, the street's a prison
  where I ride, with yielding walls, but iron
  and not to be broken through. Crown Prince I am,
  Crown Prince I must be. This is my answer to them:
  either I take the road free as a beggar,
  or from now on my life's my own. I've played
  their game, kept my intrigues hidden, held my tongue
  from comment on injustice, let myself
  be dangled like a golden calf on strings
  till I'm at the end of my tether. I married once
  to barricade the throne, a Habsburg stallion
  led to a Leopoldine filly for
  the act of royal generation. That's
  accomplished. Generation's possible
  between whichever two of opposite sex
  they lock in a room together, young enough
  to have more appetite than brain. But now
  I shall marry where I please, say what I please

in private or in public, and the storm
I rouse may drive me either up or down,
but I shall have my way.

Mary. And this ring's for me?

Rudolph. This ring's for you.

Mary. How have I earned it, Rudi?

Rudolph. I don't know. There have been other women
here in this room, a handsome company,
I give my word, and where they went afterward
concerned me only mildly. When you've gone
I hear your laughter dying down the hall
and think you're gone, but then you run in my veins
like sun on Danube water, and your hair
comes down between me and the book I write,
and I curse you for a witch. This is for boys,
this spring-sap madness, this magic in a feather,
the one red feather in one girl's dark hair,
this dreaming at windows, memory of a perfume,
this is for boys and girls, and not for me,
but with you it's mine again. And so we'll keep it.
Let them try to take it from us.

Mary. It's what I've wanted
too much to dare to wish, but now I'm trembling—
I don't know why. What will come of us, Rudi?
What will they do?

Rudolph. Why, for a time you'll hear
such a concaterwauling of horrid shrieks
you'll think Walpurgis night has broken out
in all the embassies. Little men will trot
through palace doors with black brief-cases packed
with facts and papers. Hands will be upraised,

friends estranged, lips bitten, beards gone white,
hair turned gray on diplomatic heads,
and a long growl will stem from the father walrus
to crack like thunder down the Hofburg stairs
and maybe split that curtain. Unseen hands
will write on walls—prophetic cries will rend
the midnight—vendors, likely, calling the news—
but we can't listen to stuff like that forever,
so we'll go to sleep.

Mary. I hope it comes to no more.

Rudolph. Would you be happy?

Mary. You know that.

Rudolph. And not frightened
when the wind comes up and the sacred elder statesmen
begin to rake the clinkers out of hell
to roast the two of us?

Mary. If you still want me
I won't blench at hell.

Rudolph. Then they can't hurt us.
They need me. I don't need them. But I need you—
and Q.E.D., it follows. Make your peace
at home, as best you can, for I'm not content
with these stolen interviews. We shall appear
as often as we like together.

Mary. Then—
I must tell you—there's an arrangement made—
lawyers and seals and signatures—I'm not
quite sure what all—it's covert yet, but I'm
supposed to marry—

Rudolph. Yes?

Mary. You see, I thought
    you'd tire of me. They put me up for sale,
    no doubt, for so much cash. And I said yes,
    sometime—next year, perhaps. But now I'll break it.

Rudolph. Yes, break it.

Mary. I had to tell you. You might have heard.
    Will you forgive me?

Rudolph. Who was the man?

Mary. Braganza.

Rudolph. Oh, the Duke. Well, tell the charming Duke—
    what will you tell him?

Mary. That I was passing a palace
    when a prince came out who asked me to marry him,
    and suddenly, there in the midst of winter,
    it was spring, and so I'm very sorry
    but—Rudi, Rudi, you're angry!

Rudolph. No. It's just
    the ancient masculine aversion to
    the fact of other males in the world. But break it,
    tomorrow.

Mary. Yes.—And it's true about the spring.
    I feel it like a trembling in the earth,
    this spring in winter. If I die of it
    I die of too much miracle.

Rudolph. It's not death
    to love me.

Mary. There'll be a storm—worse than you say.
    The birds' nests will come down.

Rudolph. I've never yet
  stood up before the emperor and said:
  this I intend to have! but when I do
  it may rain birds' nests in the Wienerwald
  but I shall have it.
    [*The* ARCHDUKE JOHN *of Tuscany comes in from the rear, Loschek*
    following, KOINOFF *and* SCEPS *behind them both.*]

John. It will rain birds' nest soup
  in Pesth before you rule if you can't keep
  your women out of conference!

Rudolph. Loschek!

John. Christ,
  don't blame Loschek! I walked in. We have
  an appointment here tonight—

Rudolph. No doubt you've met
  the Baroness Vetsera—the Archduke John
  of Tuscany—a man who hides his brain
  under his lack of manners.
    [*Loschek lights the candelabra and goes out.*]

John. I've heard of her.
    [*He bows.*]

Rudolph. Behind him Captain Koinoff, behind him
  Herr Sceps of the Tageblatt.
    [*Koinoff and Sceps bow. She acknowledges the salute.*]

Mary. Shall I leave you?

Rudolph. No. You can hear this.

John. Then we go back again.
  Pick up your boots, my friends, and set them down
  outside. Whatever it was we had to say

can't wait, and we can't either.
  [*He starts out.*]

Rudolph. I think you can.
  Sit down, my Salvator. The Baroness
  is in my confidence.

John. But not in mine,
  if I can help it. I've stuck my precious neck
  into a noose some dozen times this fortnight,
  all for your damn fool Highness, and got it out
  by some fool luck each time. There's such a thing
  as tempting the old lady with the shears
  just once too often.

Rudolph. The Baroness Vetsera
  will be my wife when it can be arranged.
  If you trust me, trust her.
  [*The men bow. John returns.*]

John.
    [*To Mary*]
  I beg your pardon.
    [*To Rudolph*]
  This will take some doing, though. Your current wife
  has a king to her father.

Rudolph. Yes. That's occurred to me.
  She can go home to her father.

John. Give me your hand.
  I like you better.
    [*He takes Rudolph's hand. To Mary*]
    I was burdened once
  with one of these royal frumps. She's back with mama
  and I've gone human with a chorus girl.

But you might have helped yourself to a sweeter portion
than you'll share with the prince, my dear.

Mary. I'll chance it.

John. Oh,
I don't doubt it. Where there's purple blood
a woman's apt to chance it. Come, kiss her hand,
captains and editors, before it's royal—
She'll be more distant then.
  [*Sceps and Koinoff come forward.*]

Koinoff.
  [*Kissing Vetsera's hand*]
May you be happy,
Baroness.

Mary. I thank you, Captain.

Sceps.
  [*Bending over the hand*]
May
you make him happy. For he hasn't been.

Mary. Thank you, too.

John. I have this one half-hour,
and things have happened since you galloped off
on your trumpery progress. We've talked a lot this year
of liberties, rights, broken pledges to the people,
what pressure we could bring on your father. Well,
while we talked, there were rather more forthright fellows
up and doing. It seems the Hungarians
were eighteen jumps ahead of us—they're on
the verge of a revolution.—It's not wild talk—
I don't exaggerate—the train's been laid
for such a major explosion as might lift

our sister state right out of Franz Joseph's precinct
and lay it in your lap.

Rudolph. Were these the lads
called on the carpet for circulating pamphlets
bearing my name?

John. No, no—that's another thing
though they meant business. That article you wrote
for the Tageblatt, the authorship leaked out
and several universities went berserk
in Hungary—you know, boys yelling for blood,
French style, the Marseillaise, and organizing
under the Rudolph banner. The pedagogues
were scandalized, but their innocents ran wild,
got out of hand.

Rudolph. And so they were expelled?

John. Right.

Rudolph. And that ends it.

John. For the children, yes—
but not for some others. Sceps, relate.

Sceps. Your Highness,
you know how carefully I've preserved my head,
believing, as I do, that a head's essential
even to a journalist. Your father's way
with traitors is a mild decapitation,
minus publicity. And I want to live
and raise my family and use my voice
on the side of justice, so I've walked warily
and I'm alive. But after this upheaval
in the universities, when it had all died down,
a young Hungarian noble came to see me
here in Vienna, and questioned me point blank

about your writings and yourself. I told him
what I thought safe, and when he thought it safe
he talked to me. He told me what we knew,
that Hungary's sick of the Empire, sick of your father,
ready for fireworks.—He is himself the head
of a band of young aristocrats, all sworn
to separate from Vienna or die trying,
and they don't expect to die. They mean to win;
they've organized by cities, laid their plans—
they're ready to strike now—and what he wanted
was to get word to you. They've set themselves
to make you king of Hungary. Oh, yes.
Koinoff and I went off to Buda-Pesth
to look them over, and it's true—the town's
like a hive ready to swarm—with a royal word
to lead them they'd be on the wing tonight—
tomorrow—when you say.

Rudolph. And your advice, Sceps?

Sceps. This is one time, Your Highness,
when I would risk my head. I've fought oppression
all my lifelong, and got nowhere, your father
being the man he is. We might at least
see an enlightened and liberal Hungary
break off from Austria.

Rudolph. Tell me the name
of this young noble.

Sceps. Szogyeny. You know him.

Rudolph. Yes.
And Captain Koinoff?

Koinoff. I'm somewhat less dismayed
by the word treason, Highness, than Herr Sceps,
who has a family and a paper. I

have nothing but a life that I'd exchange
for, say, a thought more freedom in the world—
and we won't get it while the emperor
sits where he sits in comfort.

Rudolph. As for the Archduke,
    I know his mind.

John. God knows I've nothing to lose
    but a starveling dukedom and a gangling neck,
    whereas you have imperial prospects, likewise
    an imperial rack of bones on which to hang
    a crown if you should get one. But your crown
    won't be worth having if you wait long for it,
    in my opinion. Five or six more years
    as things go now and the Habsburg coronets
    will rate with barrel-hoops on the market.—This
    is not our plot, this blaze in Hungary;
    it burst out ready made; it's real, it's hot,
    it's simple; it began when your mother took
    her first trip to their capitol, and begged
    some mitigation of the penalties
    your father laid on independent speech
    when he was young and brash. She got her way
    because he was in love, and since that time
    the Magyars worship her and you because
    they think you're two of a kind. No doubt you are,
    and you could give them the government they want
    and they'd follow you through brass. But take it now
    or never; a revolution grows like fruit
    and you pluck it when it's ripe or not at all.
    It won't keep on the tree.

Rudolph. You think it's ripe?

John. I know it is.

Rudolph. What would you have me do?

John. Talk with Szogyeny.

Rudolph. And then I'd be committed.

John. No. Not at all.

Rudolph. How does your word go, Mary?

Mary. You shouldn't ask me.

Rudolph. Why?

Mary. I know too little.

John. It's pretty plain if you two want to break loose
and live together, this is your chance for it.
They won't allow it here.

Rudolph. But you flatter me,
you lads, when you assume that if I ruled
the Magyars they'd be compensated for
a war, a bloody war—yes, and a lost one—
with a loss of liberties, and the fees imposed
by victors on the vanquished. I don't list
my set of bones and necessary features
among the major risks—but as a fact
I fancy them as they grow, all in one piece,
and I'd fain, fain keep them so.

John. Then I'm off for Rome
and a boat, and the South Seas! Save your fat neck
and I'll save mine!

Rudolph. If your nobility
implies that what you've told me will go further
you hardly do me justice. I'll be silent.
Yes, if the project smelled a little less
of the moon and more of the earth, I might be tempted
to listen further.

Koinoff. It's not lunacy,
   Your Highness, truly. As a student of tactics
   I should say, with the disposition of troops
   as it was three days ago, when I left Buda,
   there's little room for doubt that we could snatch
   control of Hungary. It just so happens
   that three of this pledged band we told you of
   are generals—two of them in command
   of two main key positions. A sudden movement
   made by night and both the capital cities
   would be ours, the approaches under our guns,
   and all Austria couldn't budge us.

John. You will write,
   you will talk, you will singe the old man's beard
   with words, but when we need an eagle dropping
   like thunder on the lambs, you perch on your eyrie,
   in other words your rump, and gaze at the sun
   and make snide comments on the smell of the moon
   around our enterprise! You talk to soldiers,
   and it's you that's moonstruck! Back through recorded time
   no prince was ever offered such a kingdom
   on such a platter—they had to fight for theirs,
   the Alexanders and the rest!

Rudolph. I'm not
   an Alexander. What he stood for slipped
   down the black hills in a very bloody sunset
   when the first Napoleon died. There are two reasons
   why I might wish to rule in Hungary;
   let us look at them calmly. First, if the empire
   drifts as it's drifting now, it will smash up
   and I'll be left nothing to rule. Second, if I
   were king I might inaugurate reforms
   which I've worked all my life for, and which might

be in time to stave off ruin. Well, they're both
fallacious, both these reasons. If I seize
on Hungary, there'll be a war, and all reform
wiped out for a decade, what advance we've planned
toward tolerant government will be ridden down
not only in Austria, but by my orders
in Hungary, and the empire will break up
for the same sweet reasons we have now—dragoons
on every peasant's back—the forms of law
with absolutism behind them. Add to that
that I, on whom you pin your hopes of freedom
would go the way of all the Habsburgs, lose
my liberal principles one by one, be driven
to give them up to hold a realm together,
and once committed to the adventure, doomed
to be my father over again, I'd catch
at desperate expedients, fill the gaps
in the falling walls with more and more lives of men;
acts of oppression, made to stiffen the line,
would harden into policies, we'd mix
our mortar out of the shambles of the dead
to build new bastions where more men might die
defending me, and my throne! If you're a soldier
you should know this.

John. Have you read in history
of any age when men have not been forced
to fight for freedom?

Sceps. There are times, Your Highness,
when the means are rendered gracious by the end,
though the means be evil. No war lasts forever,
nor would you change so much.

Rudolph. And that's fallacy!
A government will end as it begins,

and if it builds on slaughter it will stand
on slaughter till it falls!

Sceps. But they all begin so!

Rudolph. And they all end so! But I'll not begin
with murder that breeds murder to the end,
and whip my conscience into a corner with
"But this was needed for the ultimate good
of my dear subjects." When this same ultimate good
is but to die in a corner with my conscience
to make me a dull king! For no other purpose,
for nothing would be gained!

John. Why, then you mean
that men should sit and bleat because the butchers
have sharp knives, like a batch of calves and lambs
in the slaughter-yard! Bleat and then run away
to get their throats slit later!

Rudolph. It sounds to you
like cowardice, and it may be all thinking
has the effect of making us less apt
to spit at danger. Insofar as he thinks
a man is much more cowardly than a lion,
but he may live longer, may even get his way
more surely. Something a soldier wouldn't know,
but I offer it.

John. You have a plan?

Rudolph. Why only
this—that I know a bad plan when I see it,
and I'd rather wait. There have been instances
of men who stalked the forces of the dark
and caught them napping, men in whom indirection
and a long patience stood them in better stead

than force of arms. I'm not a patient man,
but I'm trying to learn patience.

John. By God, you've learned it!

Rudolph. Not yet I haven't—but you give me practice,
with your half cock schemes! I tell you I've looked beyond you
and caught a vision of what a man might do
if he were king. And having that vision in me
I've set myself to make myself a man
and unlearn kingliness, shed it like the rag
it is, till a king stands up a man, but a man
with power to make men free!

Mary. May I speak now,
now that I've listened, Rudolph?

Rudolph. Yes.

Mary. I've heard
you talk of danger, all of you, but it seems
you don't know what the word means. It means dying—
cruelly—dungeons without air.—For Rudolph,
if one least whisper of this goes beyond
the room, who could answer for it, who could guess
how long he'd live? You say we might be happy
in Hungary. It's not true. The emperor
watches these things, and knows them before they happen,
and hears them in the walls!

   [*There is a knock at the door.*]

Rudolph. Loschek!

   [*Loschek enters, crosses to the right, opens the door and steps out for
   a moment. He returns somewhat shaken.*]

Loschek. Your Highness,
the emperor is here and wishes to see you.

Rudolph. Very well.
> [*He dismisses his guests with a gesture.*]

Loschek. And asks, particularly
that your friends remain here with you. For he wishes
to see them also.

Rudolph. Good. My friends remain.
Will you open the door for the emperor?
> [*Loschek opens the door, bowing.* FRANZ JOSEPH *enters, dusty and humble.* TAAFE *follows.*]

Franz Joseph. I intrude
at a ghoulish hour, my son. This end of the night's
for revelling when we're young. I too kept revel
late, in my day, and understand it—yes,
and grieve to interrupt you. When your years
begin to dwindle like the coins a child
takes in his hand to carnival, you'll know
why days are precious to me, till I work
long in the night, and break in on your game
with what seems deadly urgent.

Rudolph. You're quite welcome,
Your Majesty. And we're not, as you call it,
revelling. A listener might have guessed
that we were serious.

Franz Joseph. A symposium!
Well, I can't add to that. My thinking's done.
We get that over early, we of the Habsburgs,
I'm afraid, and then we settle down
to take things as they come. They come so fast
there's little time for thinking.

Rudolph. Am I in error
or did you ask that these my guests remain
to hear our conference?

Franz Joseph. It's no conference!
   I merely wished to see you and your guests—
   these guests you have. No blenching, gentlemen!
   Be easy! I don't ask you why you're here
   nor what's been said! God's love, we talk a lot
   back in our twenties when our heads are light
   with such a lack of birthdays!

Rudolph. Do you wish
   to make the acquaintance of those present?

Franz Joseph. No—
   I know them. We won't spend our time in greetings
   but say what we came to say. I have in hand
   a copy of your missive to the Pope,
   sent without consultation. May I ask
   the meaning of it?

Rudolph. I thought the meaning plain.

Franz Joseph. You wish to marry again?

Rudolph. I do.

Franz Joseph. Your friends
   have heard of this from you?

Rudolph. They have.

Franz Joseph. But I—
   I have not. You are aware, of course,
   that marriages within the Habsburg line
   are subject to imperial control
   without exception?

Rudolph. Yes.

Franz Joseph. It should be apparent
   that you have made your prayers to the wrong throne.

This is a temporal matter. One in which
I take an interest. One that concerns the state
which I have undertaken, under God,
to lead and guide, while I have strength to do it,
and which I must not suffer to be torn
by minor loves and whims.

Rudolph. This is no whim,
sir, and no minor love.

Franz Joseph. I thought it was.
Your pardon. Where has your fancy fallen then,
in its latest phase?

Rudolph. Outside the conventions, sir.
I've chosen the Baroness Vetsera.
[*The Emperor bows to Mary.*]

Franz Joseph. Yes.—
And so I had supposed. And I must still
be blunter than I like. It's known that you've
received the lady's favors in advance
of bell and candle. Or at least your wife
has so informed the cardinal. These things
are winked at. You will tire of her, and she,
I hope, will tire of you. Play out your play.
As for divorce and marriage to her, that
I utterly refuse. A child in arms
should have more foresight.

Rudolph. If Your Majesty
will fix it in your mind that we are not
quite children here, it may be possible
to find some common ground on which our wills
can meet! I am not sorry for this visit.
For I have wished to tell you for some time
what I have in mind to do.

Franz Joseph. You'd have been wiser.

Rudolph. Not only in regard to my divorce,
    but in a graver matter. For my wife,
    I was too much a child when I allowed
    your word to bed me with a well-intentioned
    but very dull young princess. Being grown,
    and somewhat more, I shall arrange details
    of this sort for myself.

Franz Joseph. Forgive me.—And
    as to the graver matter you speak of?

Rudolph. Why,
    this Austria, this kingdom of the east,
    the Oestereich, you govern it, you bred
    this son of yours, myself, to govern it,
    set me to some five hundred tutors, one
    behind another, till I'd crammed my skull
    with usage and prerogatives and law,
    till I was read blind on usages and trash
    and like a fool I turned to drink, or women—
    the easy women you presented me
    to cut my man's teeth on, and keep me quiet
    when I was less than docile. Now I'm sick
    of this your training, and I've spewed it up,
    and it's not pretty what was stored inside
    my carcass. What have I found instilled in me
    to make me king—to fit me to be king—?
    the morals of a wolf in a court of wolves
    and bitches, such a pride in decorations
    as might become an ape, no truth, no honor,
    no faith in a man's word or a woman's, stealth
    and craft in brigandage, hyena's appetites
    for flattery that smells, resentment of
    all honesty lest it should cut too deep

and show me what I am, the tongue of a bootblack
licking out coins, but underneath a cold
analytical fury, a knowledge that all friends
are dangerous, all men enemies—

Franz Joseph. But thus—
thus is mankind, at heart.

Rudolph. This is myself
and you—no other man in the world excepting
those who are trained like you and me to rule
this outpost of disaster, Europe!

Franz Joseph. Well,
kings do not grow on bushes. They are made
as well as born, like poets. In the process
if they must pass through fire, like steel the blade
is sharper for it. And harder.

Rudolph. Sharp and hard,
and withered at the entrails, like a headsman
bred up to deal out death, and never flick
an eyelid with his shoes awash in blood
from crying children!

Franz Joseph. What child have I sent to death?

Rudolph. Too many!
    [*A pause.*]

Franz Joseph. May I ask that you state briefly
what meaning you may wish me to attach
to these hot cries from your heart? For you do mean them—
but I have not understood.

Rudolph. If it were quite plain
to me, I might make it so to you. But I wish

to leave the court, live like a commoner, choose
some obscure village where I'll touch the earth
from time to time without these damnable footmen
to spread rugs on it. I want no guards round me,
no authority, no rank; I want to sink
my roots outside this hot-house, where I'm kept
at even temperatures and if I joke
all men laugh like madmen. Because I had
a brain one time, but under this contagion
of flattery and power and sycophance
a brain can't live. I break down cell by cell,
day by day, toward that quick ulcerous growth
men call a king, a tumor on the lives of men,
with no other function than to spread, grow and eat,
rot into the body politic, spraddle out,
a witless fungus, a running sore, an evil
on what men have and are!

Franz Joseph. And you would take
this lady with you to the obscure village
for contact with the soil?

Rudolph. I would.

Franz Joseph. But then—
you would return?
Rudolph. If ever I were needed
I would return.

Franz Joseph. Do you not comprehend
that knowledge, skill and use are necessary
in managing a realm? An untried horseman
on an unbroken colt might yet stick on,
but Austria, where we ride wild horses tandem,
Austria would trample down an unpracticed rider
before he was well mounted.

Rudolph. And is this practice
  that I get now?

Franz Joseph. Count Taafe and I are here
  tonight to ask that, from tonight, you take
  a place on one of those hard stools that face
  his desk, and share our councils. We're not young,
  the Count and I. We need you as apprentice
  to take the business over when an old king
  says goodnight to an old kingdom.

Rudolph. Then—
  I shall seem most ungrateful, but it's true
  that I would rather never reign at all
  than reign as you have reigned.

Franz Joseph. We need new blood,
  a fresh voice, modern ways. What you have to say,
  we'll listen to it.

Rudolph. My first advice would be
  to grant autonomy to Hungary,
  open the franchise to all men of age
  to vote, rescind restrictions on free speech
  and press throughout the empire, wipe out clean
  all laws that make political crime, swing open
  the gates of political prisons. Sign away
  to parliament the power to make and change
  all laws, keep for yourself executive
  and advisory functions.

Franz Joseph. You have read too much.
  This is an empire, not a democracy.
  No king has ever given till he must
  what you ask me to toss away.

Rudolph. Our Habsburg house
  has been a cancer on mankind, a fluke

that eats till the host dies! Its power's cancerous,
destroying what it lives on, yes, and itself,
as it's destroyed your brain and eats at mine
to make me also what all emperors
have been, blind parasitic poisonous mouths
sucking at arteries. When you came to the throne,
the day you came to power, you signed and sealed
four hundred warrants of execution, death
to four hundred men, your enemies. Since then
you have continued as that day began,
feeding your strength on blood, your tentacles
sinking in deeper, spreading out further, till
no man dare whisper in an empty room
lest you should reach and touch him. And what for?
To build for you an arrogant machine
in middle Europe that will feel its way,
crushing and grinding men, to a larger greed,
more tributary lands, extensions of
degenerating tissue and disease
of which you make the center! This machine
is under way, and moves colossally
inch by inch, and every inch it crawls
it nears a precipice over which we'll go
and all of Europe with us!

Franz Joseph. And now indeed
    I understand you, though your flux of figures
    takes some unravelling. Still my dull old head
    asks further enlightenment. How would one rule better
    if one ruled better?

Rudolph. As if the lives of men
    were precious things, as if men's happiness
    was precious as your own. Under your hand
    men tend toward maggots, with like mouths and brains

as grow in their masters—such cheese-loving souls
that one could curse the high permitting stars
that give them leave to crawl! For your machine
has but one purpose, to iron and discipline
till men and lives are so much mud and death
in a game in which the stakes are mud and death
for enemies and friends!

Franz Joseph. And under your rule
there would be no national rivalries, no wars,
no enmities?

Rudolph. Who gains by wars but the kings?
Let the people choose war or peace.

Franz Joseph. But there's no choice.
There was a time when plagues and famines kept
the populations down, but in our wisdom
we have dispensed with famines and with plagues,
and nations press against their boundaries
incontinent, spawning more children on both sides,
till they knock the chips from one another's shoulders
and snatch the food from one another's mouths
and fight for standing room. Those who fight best
will live, and those who will not fight will die.
Shall we choose to die? Will you choose it when you're king?
The kaiser of Germany is just your age,
or nearly, William the Second, a crafty boy
but not your equal. What he dreams there in Prussia
is dominating Europe. His machine
is building up like ours. The time will come
when he will set his foot down on your lines
and two great empires, equal in wealth and men,
will lock in one mortal year. Your destiny
is war, not peace, our Rudolph against their William,
our Habsburg against their Hohenzollern. Then

the outcome hangs on who's the better man,
and there the Habsburgs have it. Not in my time
has any prince in Europe shown a promise,
a quickness, a grace, an aptness in all arts
of war and peace, such as in you, my son,
recalls an ancient glory. It rests with you
whether Austria shall live.

[*A pause. There is a clatter of rifle-butts on the floor outside.*]

A Voice.

[*Outside*]

Halt!

Another Voice.

[*Outside*]

You must wait here, madame.

A Third Voice.

[*Outside*]

The emperor is here, and you must wait.

Elizabeth.

[*Outside*]

The emperor is here—and I must wait?
I am the Empress Elizabeth, if you please,
and I will not wait.

The Third Voice.

[*Outside*]

Let her pass.

[*Loschek has slipped in from the inner rooms. At a nod from Rudolph
he opens the door. Elizabeth enters. The men bow. Rudolph
goes to her, bending over her hand.*]

Rudolph. You are welcome, mother.

Elizabeth. Thank you.
  [*To Franz Joseph*]

I came to bring a word from you to Rudolph,
but you're here before me.
  [*Loschek goes within.*]

Franz Joseph. I've little more to say,
  and I'll be gone.—When a man's old as I am,
  suddenly all he wagered on his youth,
  his dreams, what he tried to do, transfer themselves
  to the person of his son. You may not love me;
  whether I love you I don't know, it may
  mean much or little, this clutching at the throat
  where you're concerned. But surely what I've dreamed
  and hoped, and poured my passion and my days
  to serve and rescue, these are holy things:
  the honor of the Habsburgs' thousand years,
  which now devolves on you, the circle of ground
  which we call Austria, held toward east and west
  through many bloody, endless, desperate wars
  down to this hour. These you must help me keep.
  And you must take my word that keeping them
  requires you keep your name quite clear and free
  of slander, such as would come of this divorce
  and contemplated marriage. You must not
  impugn your place. You must not leave the court
  for mad *al fresco* venturing. It's fatal
  ten thousand different ways. And so I ask
  your word on both these matters.

Rudolph. You ask my word
  that I'll not leave Vienna, will not divorce
  my wife, will not remarry?

Franz Joseph. Yes.

Rudolph. It's easy
    to say that for the honor of our race,
    and to preserve our fatherland, men's blood
    must be poured down the old dynastic rat-hole
    as in the past. I say if that were true
    I'd have no interest in the government,
    nor in our fatherland, nor the tapestry
    of wars and madness our mad ancestors
    the Habsburgs wove, and in which their acts and features
    are doubtful decorations. What's the way out,
    how men are to save themselves from repetitions
    of that same tapestry in still more wars
    and blood down the same damned rat-hole, I don't know;
    but I might find out, in some other atmosphere
    than this. I shall leave the court. The Baroness
    goes with me where I go. And I shall ask,
    publicly, for a divorce.

Franz Joseph. I'm very sorry.

Rudolph. I'm sorry that we must differ.

Franz Joseph. I'm very sorry
    that to maintain much more than discipline
    I must interfere with your wishes. I know this lady
    better than you do. She must be shut away.
    Oh, in her mother's house, where she'll feel at home;
    and to put her more at ease, perhaps her jailor
    should be the man she's pledged to marry.

Rudolph. Sir,
    you grow childish.

Franz Joseph. When we deal with children,
    with wilful children, we must sometimes adopt
    a childish method. I have known your mother

to glance off at these tangents in her time,
and thank me later for restraints.

Elizabeth. A woman's
easily broken. Take care how you anger Rudolph.
You won't break him so easily.

Franz Joseph. My dear,
where our treasure is—you've read it in Holy Writ.
Rudolph will stay in Vienna.

Rudolph. From this hour
I do and say and go as I please.

Franz Joseph. Why then—
it's as I said. Taafe, the guard was needed,
and you were right after all.

Taafe. Shall I call them?

Franz Joseph. Yes.
[*Taafe steps to the door and opens it.*]

Rudolph. The royal guard!

Franz Joseph. I do regret it, Rudolph.

Rudolph. You will regret it.

Taafe. Come in. You're to make an arrest.
[Two or Three Soldiers *enter, an* Officer *following.*]

Franz Joseph. This lady goes with us.

Rudolph. Your Majesty,
this is opera bouffe! To arrest her in my rooms!

Franz Joseph. It will not be printed. You may trust our discretion,
Herr Sceps and me. Even the Archduke John
will curb his tongue. You were lately in Buda-Pesth,
were you not, sir?

John. No, Your Majesty.

Franz Joseph. Good. We'll say nothing
of that, nor of this either.
  [*To Mary*]
Will you come?

Rudolph. She'll stay where she is.

Franz Joseph. Oh, now I beg of you,
no words, no violence!
  [*To Mary*]
  My guest for the evening
only, and then your mother's. As I've said
I know you better than Rudolph.

Mary. Yes. I'll go.
  [*She looks once at Rudolph, then walks out through the soldiers. The
  Officer and the soldiers go with her.*]

Rudolph. You count on your gray hair
and greasy words too much! You've never seen me
angry—but by your own everlasting God
you may find such a change in me as we'll
regret—both of us—if you let her walk between soldiers
three steps farther—!

Franz Joseph. I should think less of you
and the metal in you if you showed no temper
at such a moment. Be angry. It will pass,
and you'll think better of it. There are matters
much more important than the boiling-point
of turbulent princes. You spat out your defiance
lightly, across my face. No man, since I
was crowned, has spoken so to me, nor will
and go unpunished.

Rudolph. But I have, and will,
 and will again! What do you gain by this?

Franz Joseph. Time—and your presence
 here in Vienna—on which we set a value.
 But mainly time—the only cure I know
 for adolescent ills. I wish you well.
 I'm cruel to be kind. But when to be kind
 I must be cruel, I use no half-measures.
 Reflect on that. And when you're cooler try
 if there's a way to my clemency.
   [*He bows and goes out with Count Taafe.*]

Rudolph. This is the ultimate in degradation—
 to come here ready with a squad of soldiers
 and take her like a criminal! It's second childhood,
 and empty posturing.

Elizabeth. It wasn't empty
 once when a squad of soldiers visited
 my lodging in Madiera. Oh, it's known
 that I was then a rebel, rebel enough
 to fall very much in love. The man was Imry.
 We thought we'd kept it secret, but this rank
 of guardsmen came—in their comic opera fashion—
 without warrant or warning, and what was done with him
 I never knew. Perhaps the Baroness
 will not be seen again.

Rudolph. But that's not possible!

Elizabeth. It's happened. Oh, to make a hole in the earth
 and lay an unwanted body in it, that's
 quite possible. What we call civilization
 is built on dead men's silence.

Rudolph. What can be done?

Elizabeth. Nothing. He has his way.

Rudolph. But not with me!

Elizabeth. I hope not.

John. Now will you take this Hungary
      we offer you, and pay him back in his coin,
      or will you sit here still in your fine detachment,
      contemplating destiny?

Rudolph. What in God's name
      do I want with Hungary?

John. Make her queen of it,
      make yourself king. Look, Rudolph, if you strike
      before he's warned we'll have the Baltazzi palace
      and Mary out of it and be off across
      the border, to a new kingdom, while he's still
      awaiting your apology!

Rudolph. We have
      no arms, no plans, no men—

John. I'll find you fifty
      within six hours!

Elizabeth. And now I could almost hope.

Rudolph. For what?

Elizabeth. That he'll be broken.

Sceps. He has information.
      He knew we'd been in Buda.

Elizabeth. He has little.
      He sent me here with a bit of cold advice
      for Rudolph's ear, that some of his hot-head friends
      might find their heads in danger.

Sceps. That's enough.

Elizabeth. No, no! It only means he plays for time
   and isn't ready for you.

Rudolph. It's a madman's scheme,
   incredible as a nightmare. No sane man
   would believe it might be tried, or might succeed,
   unless doors open of themselves and walls
   come down on hinges. Yet it may be they do
   after this nightmare we've lived through, his guards
   set in the halls, and an emperor at large
   with paranoia. Find your fifty men,
   and we'll raid the Baltazzi palace.

John. There's fire in the man!

Rudolph. Do you think I'm tame?

Sceps. I'll drop out. I've given
   too many hostages.

John. Save yourself and your paper.
   You say we'll raid the palace—and after that
   what happens?

Rudolph. What else could happen—then we'll try
   for Hungary.
      [*John takes Rudolph's hand.*]

John. Koinoff, come in. Your hand on this.

Koinoff. Oh, count on me.

John. The devil drink his eyes
   that breaks this pact.

Sceps. Put me in too. Good God,
   we die sometime.

John. That's better. That makes our circle.

Rudolph. And now I set my hand to it I'll go
    as far as your best madmen. If he wants war
    he shall have war. Mother, you're one of us.
      [*Elizabeth steps toward the circle of men and then pauses.*]

Elizabeth. I wish I might. But my heart's in your enterprise
    too far to touch it with my hand. The lips
    and hands I've aided in rebellion, they're
    all cold. There's an old fatality in me
    that I outlive all those with whom I league
    against him. Make your compact, you who are young
    and may be lucky. I am a wraith of things
    long dead and buried. I must not burden you
    with griefs past sounding.
      [*She turns to go.*]

CURTAIN

THE MASQUE OF KINGS

ACT TWO

ACT II

SCENE I

SCENE: *The following evening in the study of Franz Joseph. This time the room is fully revealed and is seen to be of ample size and exquisitely furnished. An inner door at the left leads to the Emperor's apartments, the outer door is at the right. Near the entrance at the right sits the* MAID *who has been seen previously in Rudolph's room. The* BARONIN VON NEUSTADT *stands near her.*

The Baronin. My dear, it would hardly do if you were to be found sitting when the Emperor entered, would it, now?

The Girl. No, madam.
   [*She rises.*]

The Baronin. On the other hand, the Baronin von Neustadt, for ineffable reasons, may be found seated, even by royalty, on condition that she rises immediately to meet such an august occasion.
   [*She sits.*]

The Girl. Yes, madam.

The Baronin. Pardon me these hornbook lessons in deportment, but as you rise higher in the state you will find them more and more to your advantage, perhaps even obligatory. You have not been summoned previously to this Holy of Holies?
   [*The Girl is silent.*]
There—the fault was mine—you must not violate a confidence. —And yet, I know your business here very well, since it's the same as my own, perfidious wretch that I am. I sell information for pin money, my husband being sometimes a little to the windward of lavish, and you do the same for bread and butter— therefore your secret's safe with me and mine with you.

The Girl. I have no secret, madam.

The Baronin. Excellent! And so dewily, so fragrantly, so honestly said! And so we wait here cheek by jowl, petticoat to

65

petticoat, the above-stairs smothering its knowledge in words, the below-stairs in silence—but still in perfect understanding, baronin and parlor-maid, for next to death there is no leveller of classes like espionage.—But what levels us is that we find it a rather despicable business, and despise ourselves and each other in our hearts.

The Girl. Despise ourselves?

The Baronin. Don't you?

The Girl. No.

The Baronin. No? Come, come, my dear, there are a half-dozen of us waiting to clear up some minor doubt that balks the imperial will in respect to Rudolph. A very nasty occupation; and we take money for it.

The Girl. I hate him.

The Baronin.

[*Rising*]

Truly? But then you have a reason. No doubt he has given reasons, though none to me. No, my interest is purely mercenary, and I sink below you in my estimation. Occupy the chair, my dear, and I shall stand.

The Girl. Thank you, madam.

[*She remains standing.*]

The Baronin. Strange, strange, how a woman will love a man for robbing her of youth and filling her with innumerable children, while she will hate him forever if he gives her back to herself with her good looks intact and only a memory of pleasure to remind her of him! There, there—I meant nothing by it. My remarks, as usual, are for the ambient air, and by no stretch treasonous.

[*The inner door opens, and Count Taafe enters.*]

Taafe. You will oblige me by waiting in the anteroom for a moment, Baronin von Neustadt. I have a word to say to this young woman.

The Baronin. Surely, Taafe, surely. Ah, my child, you will go far. You already take precedence.
[*She goes out right.*]

Taafe. What was she saying to you?

The Girl. Only, sir, that she knew my business very well, because it was the same as her own.

Taafe. Very true, and quite democratic of her, though indiscreet. However, she's a mistress of indiscretion, and makes it serve her ends. Whatever you do don't attempt to emulate her in that direction.

The Girl. No, sir.

Taafe. So far, and so far as I know, you've been close-mouthed under strong temptation. Remain so, and we shall continue to be pleased.

The Girl. Yes, sir.

Taafe. Your instructions this evening are very simple. There is, or is likely to be, somewhere in the Prince Rudolph's apartments, a list of Hungarian officers and noblemen. If you can lay your hand on it, copy what you can without risk, or memorize as much of it as you have time for. The list may not be there at all, as I say. Someone else may have it, or he may carry it upon his person. But we need it quickly and desperately, and you may happen on it if you try.

The Girl. Yes, sir.

Taafe. That's all.

The Girl. Thank you, sir.

> [*She goes out.* A Little Man in a Cap *enters.*]

Taafe. I suppose you know, Rauscher, that the Crown Prince was in his apartments last night while you were amusing yourself at the Tzigan dancer's?

Rauscher. I followed his domino, sir, and it was a man of just his build. What's more, he must have been imitating the prince's walk. You'd have sworn to it yourself.

Taafe. I hope you know who it was?

Rauscher. I know now. It was Bratfisch, the coachman.

Taafe. As it happens it doesn't matter this time, because we had other information. But for the future, you have your instructions. Don't be misled again.

Rauscher. No, sir.

Taafe. That's all.

> [*Rauscher bows and goes out. The Baronin reenters.*]

The Baronin. Your most humble servant.

Taafe. My dear baronin, your extremely agile and provocative tongue may sometime dig you a bear-pit so deep and wide that God and man will not be able to extricate you from it.

The Baronin. Ah, luckless that I am, what have I said now?

Taafe. You'll find it just as well to avoid communication with others of our—shall I say our under-cover staff? As you must be aware, ideas are poisonous to the unsophisticated mind, and you are unfortunately not devoid of certain helter-skelter philosophic concepts—

The Baronin. Oh, you do me too much honor!

Taafe. Concepts of a corrupting character which pervade your very charming conversation, and which do you no harm, but might well pervert a simple faith or taint an untutored devotion.

The Baronin. I love that.

Taafe. Curb yourself, my dear baronin. No further remarks of any kind to the little serving-maid. It may not have occurred to you, but there are only two ways out of the ranks you entered when you consented to employ yourself on our little missions. One of them is an honorable discharge after years of undeviating and scrupulous fidelity. The other we shall not speak of, but it would entail the loss of many things which at present make life endurable to you—first and least among them your freedom to go and come.

The Baronin. And I may not resign?

Taafe. There is no third alternative. And let me say that the mere suspicion that you wish to resign is enough to place you in a most precarious position.

The Baronin. I have no wish to do so. I merely asked.

Taafe. Good.—The rest is business. You have seen the Baroness Vetsera?

The Baronin. Yes.

Taafe. She is still rather disconsolate, no doubt?

The Baronin. I should guess so, though you will agree that she has her reasons for being fairly monosyllabic toward me—knowing me as she does.

Taafe. There is no possible manner in which she might correspond with Rudolph?

The Baronin. There's but one door to her room, dear count. It's locked, and the Duke of Braganza keeps the key. No servants are allowed to enter, her mother being thoroughly on your side in this business.

Taafe. The Duke, I hope, is a jealous man?

The Baronin. Jealous, tyrannical and exacting. He will make her an excellent husband. He is, for the moment, an excellent jailor.

Taafe. It was he who admitted you to see her?

The Baronin. At your request, yes.

Taafe. It would be annoying if she hanged herself, or threw herself from the window.

The Baronin. Oh, but she's young, passionate and full of hope. She will be quite as passionate in another direction once she's married to the Duke.

Taafe. These women are cynical about each other.

The Baronin. We have reason to be.

[*Franz Joseph enters from the left. Taafe turns to him deferentially, the Baronin bows.*]

Franz Joseph. Have you heard from Koinoff?

Taafe. No, Your Majesty. I've expected him since three o'clock.

Franz Joseph. Will you ask the baronin whether she knows of any faint suspicion that Captain Koinoff may be less than wholehearted in our cause?

Taafe. You know, my dear baronin, that Koinoff has been entrusted with a delicate commission in connection with Rudolph. He has appeared admirably diligent and we had a report from him this morning, but now, just when we stand in dire need of further information, he has failed an appointment to meet us, and is all of six or seven hours behind-hand—with no word from him.

The Baronin. Oh, but he may be entangled in such a fashion that it would give his hand away to leave—

Taafe. True, but for seven hours, and when we depend on him utterly.—How much did you know of him when he was first recommended to us?

The Baronin. Only that he was clever, needed money, and looked honest.

Taafe. But now we find that he was employed in Berlin under Prince Bismarck before coming to Vienna—in some quasi-secretarial capacity. He left Berlin under a fairly noxious cloud. In fact, it's probable that he's had a startlingly wide experience in double-tonguing and quick exits. That his schooling was with the Jesuits has not added to our confidence.

The Baronin. I had no notion of all this.

Taafe. When it's added that the Vetsera girl was also your recommendation you will comprehend why we grow slightly uneasy about the character of your friends.

The Baronin. But that—nobody could foresee. She fell in love.
   [*There is a knock at the door, and a Servant enters.*]

The Servant. Captain Koinoff is here, Count Taafe.

Taafe. Ah, that alters matters. Send him in at once.
   [*The Servant goes out.*]

We excuse the baronin, thoroughly re-instated in our good opinion.

The Baronin. Exonerated by accident, Your Majesty—in the casual manner of this world we live in.

Franz Joseph. My dear, the appalling amount of accident in the best-governed dominions is hardly flattering to a king.
   [*The Baronin bows and goes out.*]

And yet we must get rid of this woman. Her tongue is like an open razor in the hands of a child.

[*Koinoff enters and bows.*]

Koinoff. Your Majesty—Count Taafe—

Taafe. You are late, sir.

Koinoff. Indeed I am, and I've been bleeding inwardly over it ever since the clock went past the hour.

Taafe. You have the list?

Koinoff. No. I expect to get it this evening.

Taafe. But you have gathered the most important names?

Koinoff. Only Szogyeny.

Taafe. Come, come, Captain Koinoff, you have Rudolph's entire confidence, you are acting as military advisor to the leaders, there is an all-important list of rebelling Hungarians on the table before you, and you fail to memorize one additional name.

Koinoff. But the list has not been displayed, it has not been discussed in my presence, and I can't ask for it, as you must realize.

Taafe. You could angle for it, and if you were adroit you would have got it long ago. In your capacity of tactical expert you can express doubt of their strength in the west—they will answer by identifying their allies in that region. You can demand specific information as to their support from ranking officers in Buda-Pesth—they will reply by enumerating certain members of the clique—

Koinoff. They have given that information in a general way. But there seems to be a tacit understanding among them that their confederates are to remain anonymous till they're ready to strike—

Taafe. And when will that be?

Koinoff.
  [*Smiling*]
  We plan to rescue the Baroness Vetsera from the Baltazzi palace and leave for Hungary tonight.

Taafe. A sufficiently hair-brained project.

Koinoff. And easily prevented.

Franz Joseph. But it must be apparent to you, Captain Koinoff, that before we move openly to prevent it we must have in our hands the names of my sworn enemies in Hungary. Otherwise I may never know them. And until I know them I can take no steps to forestall a much more serious thing, a major and well-planned revolution in Hungary, with or without Rudolph.

Koinoff. Yes, Your Majesty.

Franz Joseph. Then I shall expect you here with at least a portion of that list before midnight. If we have some of them we can get the rest. No doubt your heroic little band is even now in a fever of preparation?

Koinoff. Yes, it is, Your Majesty.

Franz Joseph. Then go and we shall wait for you.
  [*Koinoff bows and goes out.*]

Taafe. The movement of troops into Hungary has been taken care of. Several trains left at seven this evening and others will follow during the night. I was obliged to entrain the Seventh Corps, because no other could be got ready on short notice. It leaves Vienna almost entirely unprotected, but I felt that the emergency required it, and we run no risk here.

Franz Joseph. It may be all these things come home to roost, sometime, what we've been and done. I see them camp

round us tonight. There's a shadow of black wings
between me and the candles. Well, my ways
have not been pretty always.

Taafe. That's the voice
of a man who needs his sleep.

Franz Joseph. I could use some sleep
if I could sleep. But that's not what it is.
It's that this ruling as I've ruled is like
a child's sand castle by the sea. It stands
with flags and soldiers till the sea licks at it
gently, a little at a time, and then
in one great wash it's gone. Perhaps the tide
is due now. We've both seen it on the flats
in Hungary, and it's not turned yet.

Taafe. My king,
this is a morbid strain, and baseless. There's
no danger in these youngsters.

Franz Joseph. It's their world,
and we're old men, hanging on by our last half-hours,
alive by a legal fiction. There's something forgotten,
something we've overlooked that makes it fatal,
and I don't know what it is.

CURTAIN

ACT II

Scene 2

SCENE: *A small section of Rudolph's room, including the portrait of the Empress, the desk beneath it, and a number of chairs which have been pulled up to the desk for a study of maps and schedules.*

RUDOLPH *and* SCEPS *bend over papers under the light. Rudolph is in military uniform.*

Rudolph.

[*Reading a note*]

"She will escape. Wait for her." And you found this on your desk?

Sceps. With no envelope, just the sheet
of plain note paper.

Rudolph. Every move one makes
recorded and transmitted under ground
as if by seismograph. But it's from a friend.
It may come from her. We'll wait till midnight—
no longer.

Sceps. Shall I draw the proclamation?

Rudolph. It was Napoleon Bonaparte, the runt,
who first worked out the formula still used
for consolidating conquest. Caesar, before him,
cut him a crop of kings, and then went on,
more or less bored to discover that new kings
sprang up behind him. But the young scrub Napoleon,
with a heart like that of a cheap Swiss watch, and the brain
of a coffin salesman, set out to sell his wares
by getting one foot indoors, and then proclaiming
his stuff was free, guaranteed, and a hundred years
to pay. He tried it first in Italy,

offering liberty, also fraternity,
equality gratis, and all they had to do
was let him buckle their shoulders into a collar
and the world was theirs. Our aim is not the same,
but the formula's still good. Our first six words
in Hungary tomorrow must be these:
We come to set you free.

Sceps. But is this model
apt for your purpose, Highness?

Rudolph. If it works
when it's but a trick, it should be more effective
when we mean to carry it out. We must weld the nation
in one day, in one hour. Is policy
the peculiar possession of thieves?

Sceps. It's so considered.
But it may be superstition. I'll try a draft
and show it to you.

Rudolph. Make it brief and simple.
Brief as a boy's prayer, simple as its answer.

Sceps. I'll try it.

Rudolph. Yet at the very best, not all
will follow us. There are men in Hungary
who have no interest in our freedom. Some
who'd rather die than see their revenues
reduced three groschen. Some of them will die,
no doubt.

Sceps. My lord, I hope——

Rudolph. I know your hope.
You hope this revolution won't come down
to what the history of revolutions

predicts too clearly: a struggle for what's there
on the part of those who want it. That's my hope, too.
And yet I fear that certain men must die
if we're to win. And we must win.
  [*Loschek enters.*]

Loschek. Your Highness.

Rudolph. Yes.

Loschek. The Archduke is here with Count Joseph Hoyos.

Rudolph. Cover these papers. We'll see him at once.
    [*Loschek goes out. Sceps lays a newspaper over the confusion of maps.
    John of Tuscany comes in with Count Hoyos.*]

John. I beg your pardon, Rudolph, a visitor,
    if you have a moment's time.

Rudolph.
    [*Giving his hand to Hoyos*]
    I'm glad to see you,
    never more so.

Hoyos. God and the Archduke John
    know why I'm here. We had some talk in a corner,
    and he told me you were up. That is, the Archduke;
    so far God's said nothing.

Rudolph. Don't wait for him.
    He hasn't spoken since Moses.

Hoyos. Well, my lord,
    I don't know what's in the wind. John spoke in riddles,
    very darkly, of some black inner ring
    fed up with tyranny.

Rudolph. No doubt there are
    such groups. I'm not acquainted with them.

John. Oh,
  but Hoyos made an answer.

Rudolph. Yes?

Hoyos. I said
  that my digestion was somewhat impaired
  by the same diet. So we chatted on
  still quite obscurely, led from one thing to another,
  till I found myself led here.

Rudolph. This Salvator
  will swear to a good deal more than he'll live up to,
  and nobody minds. He's not serious.

Hoyos. I see.
  We'll wipe it out. Let's talk about the hunting.
  I shall try Mayerling this year.

John. Good God,
  I took my soundings! You can back my word
  Count Hoyos is as safe a man to talk with
  as any of us!

Rudolph. Keep your head, my cousin.
  The count is trusted by the emperor
  for excellent reasons. Likewise he commands
  the imperial troops in Vienna. I know him loyal
  as I am. If you're meditating treason
  try somewhere else.

Hoyos. This is the truth, Prince Rudolph;
  there's been but little said, but it's enough
  so that if I were colored all the way through
  like this imperial uniform, I'd buzz
  a bee in the emperor's ear, but as it is
  my insides are my own when I take my clothes off
  and probably much like yours. Whether I'm with you

or not, no man shall hear of you from me,
either now or later. We're mutually aware
of a singular danger in frankness. Drop pretence,
and I'll drop it too.

Rudolph. I've known you a long time.
I'll take your word for bond on any subject.
This is a graver matter than you think,
not to be entered lightly.

Hoyos. I'm grave enough.
And I have my grievances, Rudolph.

Rudolph. And could you
afford to lose royal favor?

Hoyos. I have lost it. I'm to lose my command.
I might get it back again, from you.

Rudolph. Our plans
don't touch Vienna.

Hoyos. Aye—aye, Buda-Pesth.
Yes, I'd be useless there. That leaves me out.

Rudolph. I thought it would.

Hoyos. But you have my good wishes, boy.
Go on and take it from him, if you can.
Only why not make a real revolution of it,
go after all or nothing?

Rudolph. We're not ready.
Hungary's organized. And add to that,
I want no more than comes to me of itself:
I make no bid for Austria.

Hoyos. That's a pity,
because you could certainly have it.

Rudolph. You think so, Hoyos?

Hoyos. Hell, I could almost give it to you myself!
Your father has no friends he doesn't pay for,
and there are installments overdue among
some folk I know.
[*Loschek enters.*]

Loschek. Your Highness was expecting the Baroness Vetsera?

Rudolph. Can she be here?

Loschek. She is here, sir.

Rudolph. Then at once—

Loschek. Yes, Highness.
[*He goes out. Mary enters.*]

Rudolph. Mary—

Mary. Don't touch me—don't touch me till I've told you—
is Koinoff here?

Rudolph. Not yet.

Mary. Then when he comes
put a knife in him! He's in the Emperor's pay,
and has been all along!

Rudolph. Koinoff?

John. Oh, no.
We went to Koinoff first. We picked him out
because he was our kind.

Mary. But I know! I know!
It wasn't easy to come and tell you this;
don't question it, and don't wait! Whatever's said
to him goes straight to the Emperor!

Rudolph. How have you learned this?

Mary. From the Baronin von Neustadt. She told me to get you word
   of that, and remind you that she'd promised once
   to be your friend. I couldn't send, so I came.
   Oh, I know it's true.

Sceps. That blocks our expedition
   before it starts.

John. She may have lied to you.
   She's not to be trusted on either side.

Mary. Oh, yes,
   in this—she is.

Rudolph. We heard that you were guarded.
   Have they let you go?

Mary. I found my way round that.
   The Duke of Braganza thinks he can trust me now.
   He's been somewhat misled.—You need never touch me,
   never, because I can feel his kisses on me,
   his fat-toad kisses, till I'll never be clean,
   never; Oh, all I'll ask of you is haste,
   lest you be too late, for he was here, this Koinoff,
   and heard the plans!
      [*Rudolph goes to Mary. She steps back.*]

      Oh, Rudi, Rudi, it's ended,
   you and me, too!

Rudolph. I think not, not you and me,
   see, thus we wipe it out, whatever it was.
      [*He kisses her.*]

   I'll take you, and let the world go. I'll maybe have to,
   for this news of yours, it brings our balloon to earth,

so much rag. It may even mean my days
as prince of the blood are over. Gentlemen,
we're warned in time so that if we're quick about it
and clever we may save the firing-squads
unnecessary labor.

John. I doubt the story,
the Koinoff story.

Hoyos. I think the lady's right.
Why were they shipping troops to Hungary
this evening?

John. Were they?

Hoyos. Yes, train-loads of them.
Nobody knew why.
    [*A pause.*]

Rudolph. If you wish to leave, Count Hoyos,
we're not very healthy company.

Hoyos. No, you're not.
    [*He rises.*]
If that snake Koinoff crawls in while I'm here
I'm damned with the rest of you.
    [*He starts out.*]
    In case you find
two or three dozen horses would come handy
for any purpose, there's a cavalry stable
near the Mall. The doors will be unlocked
and no guard set.

Rudolph. Thanks, Hoyos. We may use
some of your nags.—If any of you should wish
to leave at once, they'll watch the west roads, so—
we'd best go south for the winter. For myself,

I have an account to settle. I shall wait
a few moments more.
  [*Hoyos turns away.*]

John. So shall I.
  [*Koinoff enters through the shadow.*]

Koinoff. I give you greeting,
  gentlemen.

Hoyos. Koinoff?

Koinoff. Yes, general. It's Count Hoyos, is it not?

Hoyos. Right, right.

Koinoff. I'm unannounced, your Loschek
  waved me in, as expected.
  [*Hoyos returns.*]

Rudolph. Come, sit down,
  we need you, Captain. There's a road here, look,
  nobody seems to know.
  [*He bends over a map.*]

Koinoff. I was not aware
  Count Hoyos was one of us.

Hoyos. You sometimes find
  a red-wing among blackbirds.

Koinoff. All the better.
  Why, this road, we talked of it yesterday.
  The Baroness Vetsera!

Mary. Yes.

Koinoff. Good Lord,
  that simplifies our problem.

Rudolph. We pick things up
as we go along.

Koinoff. Yes, sir.—There was a question
about this road?

Rudolph. It shows on this one map
but not on the other three. Are you sure it's there—
for we'll need it?

Koinoff. It's a military road,
built two years ago, and never used
for commercial traffic. But it's there.

Rudolph. You have
these things at your finger tips.

Koinoff. I've studied them.

Rudolph. Hungary, too—you know it
as well as Austria.

Koinoff. Yes, sir.

Rudolph. We were speaking of you
before you came, Captain Koinoff. There's no man
among us but yourself who knows this maze
of forts and arsenals and guns. Count Hoyos
is out of it. He's studied Austria
but not the west. The rest of us grew up
with politics and statecraft. We shall want
a general we can trust, one of ourselves,
to lead the Hungarian armies. Would you accept
the commission from me?

Koinoff. Your Highness, it's beyond
my hope or my desert.

Rudolph. But would you take it?

Koinoff. I'm inexperienced in handling men—
　　except by companies.

Rudolph. But you know tactics
　　and strategy, you're acquainted with the field,
　　at least the Hungarian border?

Koinoff. Yes.

Rudolph. Would this
　　make up to you for the small weekly stipend
　　you draw from the emperor?

Koinoff. From the emperor? I?

Rudolph. You. From the emperor.

Koinoff. Surely, Prince Rudolph,
　　you know me better. Tell me who's whispered this
　　and I'll refute it.

Rudolph. It wasn't whispered, captain.
　　It's known. But we're inclined to say no more
　　about it, since we need you, and your heart's
　　on our side more than his. An old arrangement,
　　made with Count Taafe for your laundry bills,
　　it happens with lieutenants. They make out
　　perfunctory reports for a week or two,
　　then let it drop. If that was true of you
　　what of it? It's gone now.

Koinoff. It was never true.
　　Tell me who's said it!

Rudolph. It will be evident,
　　if you reflect, that though we want and need you,
　　we shall regard you with less confidence
　　if you're not open with us. I know quite well
　　it's a usual slip with these cadets. I've seen

their schoolboy writings. Come, man, make confession
and get your absolution.

Koinoff. It was years ago.
I'd almost forgotten it.

Rudolph. That's more like a man.
Then it was true?

Koinoff. Yes.

Rudolph. But you've broken it off?
You make no more reports?

Koinoff. It was as you said,
Your Highness, a schoolboy business. I'm heartily sorry
that it should trouble you now.

Rudolph. Can you explain
why troop-trains were departing from Vienna
for Hungary this evening?

Koinoff. No, I can't.
I didn't know it.

Rudolph. Then I'll tell you why.
Because a hybrid snake named Koinoff truckles
from one suite to another in this palace
conveying news! Stand away from him! We shall end
this custom of wearing swords among ophidians,
at least by one! I'm good with my rapier,
even by candle-light! Try how you are!
Quick, for we're short of time!

Koinoff. I won't fight with you!

John. I'll cut your throat, you hound!

Rudolph. Let me deal with him!—
I have a strain of cruelty in me,

and it comes out when I look at vipers. Yes,
and on you I'll turn it loose. Sit on that chair!
And now you're there let me assure you, sir,
you'll never rise from it.

Mary. Rudi!

Rudolph. Let me alone
till I've disemboweled the rat!

Koinoff. I'm innocent!
I'm not to blame!

Hoyos. There's often a use for rats,
Rudolph. Don't waste him.

Rudolph. What experiment
would you suggest?

Hoyos. Ask him what regiments
were left here to guard Vienna.

Koinoff. I can tell you!
Whatever you want to know!

Rudolph. Our adventure's done!
We have no further use for information
concerning guards and troops.

Hoyos. Our choice lies now
between a very chancy dash for the border
and the capture of Vienna. The latter sounds
more likely to succeed.

Koinoff. As God's my judge,
there are three regiments left here, and Count **Hoyos**
commands them!
    [*He points at Hoyos.*]

Rudolph. Hoyos?

Hoyos. It's past all doubt I do
    command three regiments. If that's what's left,
    and it may be, it's your city, and your kingdom.
    I make you a present of it.

John. Take it then.
    You seem to have some question in your mind.
    Boy, it's better than hanging.

Rudolph. Perhaps it is.

John. Perhaps! Perhaps! Man, the great wheel goes round—
    and we go up, and the emperor goes down!
    Seventeen's our number, and it shows!
    Quick, man, quick like a rat, rake in your fortune
    before it changes!

Sceps. We have luck at last!

Rudolph. I'm sorry they pulled me off. My fingernails
    are white to the bone with an itch for murder! I'd give
    a kingdom or two to have the carving of you
    when I remember how you came and went
    and smiled in our faces! Where was the emperor
    when you last saw him?

Koinoff. Waiting in his study.

Rudolph. For what?

Koinoff. I'd promised him a list of names,
    the Hungarian nobles.

Rudolph. Must I still let him live?

Hoyos. These rats are useful. In a war, my God,
    there's nothing like them!

Rudolph. Then stand up, and put
    your wrists behind you. Tie them together, someone.

If I should touch him he might come apart
in my hands, and lose what usefulness a rat
may have.—And so he's waiting for a list
of our Hungarian friends. We'll take it to him.
He can eat it for supper.

Hoyos. One word first! How far
do we go in this? It's safer yet to run
if we're not set to smash the whole way through
and come out on the other side!

Rudolph. What side?

Hoyos. Beyond
the emperor's power to touch us! If you leave
one shred of kingship to him, or influence,
he'll build it up so craftily, we'll all
make mincemeat for him!

Rudolph. We shall leave him nothing!
The man has one strength only, and that's to weave
his webs around you till he binds you down
with one strand after another. Let him weave!
Tonight we pitch his checkerboard in the moat
and all the pieces with it! The game's over
and we start a new one!—Pull it up till it cuts—
we want no slipping!—Step on ahead. Yes, you,
you with your arms tied.—

    [*Koinoff goes toward the hall.*]

CURTAIN

ACT II

SCENE 3

SCENE: TAAFE *and* FRANZ JOSEPH *are sitting in the study over a chess-board. Taafe moves a piece.*

Franz Joseph. Mate, then.

Taafe. What will you play?

Franz Joseph. Pawn takes knight, sir.

Taafe. I hadn't seen it. I thought you beaten.

Franz Joseph. I was.
Then suddenly it unfolded. The ancient brain's
not quite dead for sleep. We'll give our Rudolph
a run for it yet.

Taafe. It's midnight, and no news.
What shall we do?

Franz Joseph. Wait.
    [*The Servant enters.*]

The Servant. Captain Koinoff's here,
Your Majesty.

Franz Joseph. Send him in.
    [*The Servant goes out.*]

Taafe. I don't trust Koinoff.
He fancies himself.
    [*Koinoff enters, his hands behind him. Taafe leaps up.*]
    Your hands, sir! Why are your hands
behind you?
    [*Koinoff shrugs.*]

Koinoff. They're tied there.

Taafe. Tied?

Koinoff. Why, look for yourself.
I don't care for the fashion. If you'll undo them
I'll wear them somewhere else.
   [*Taafe looks out through the curtains.*]

Taafe. You're alone?

Koinoff. Not quite.
Prince Rudolph's on his way. I'm sent ahead
as avaunt courier.

Franz Joseph. Sir, explain yourself.
Has Rudolph sent you to ask audience?

Koinoff. Yes.

Franz Joseph. Then why are your wrists bound?

Koinoff. Sir, he did it,
or it was done at his order.

Franz Joseph. Unlace his hands.
You will return to Rudolph and say from me
his audience is granted. You seem to have bungled
your business badly.

Koinoff. They knew before I came,
and were ready for me.

Franz Joseph. They knew?

Koinoff. No doubt of it.
Also there's little use in sending back
because he's coming. And will enter when he likes.
And bring whom he pleases.

Taafe. There's a guard in the hall.

Koinoff. It's gone.

Franz Joseph.
   [*Roaring*]
   The guard?

Koinoff. Your Majesty, it's gone.

Franz Joseph. See what he means.
   [*Taafe steps out.*]

Koinoff. Your Majesty, I'll offend,
   whatever I do, but somehow between the time
   I left them and returned, they'd learned about me,
   yet what they sent me here to say I cannot
   and dare not say.

Franz Joseph. Deliver your message, sir.

Koinoff. I dare not, truly. In this room, where you
   are most a king, I dare not.

Franz Joseph. It's from Rudolph?

Koinoff. Yes.

Franz Joseph. He makes demands?

Koinoff. Yes.

Franz Joseph. Are you more afraid
   of Rudolph than of me? For if you're not
   why do you mention it at all? The lad
   has frightened you!
   [*Taafe returns.*]

Taafe. Your Majesty, Prince Rudolph,
   accompanied by some two or three, is here
   asking admittance.

Franz Joseph. And the guard?

Taafe. The guard
   may have been changing. But it's set as usual.
   I know the men.

Franz Joseph. The captain exaggerates.
   Who's with Rudolph?

Taafe. Herr Sceps, the Archduke John,
   and Mary Vetsera.

Franz Joseph. Vetsera? The boys are quick!
   They've been bird's nesting!

Taafe. Yes.

Franz Joseph. I'll see Prince Rudolph.
   Not the others.
        [*Rudolph enters.*]

Rudolph. You were not so delicate
   when you led an expedition into my rooms
   and over-ran us with soldiery.

Franz Joseph. Come in.
   You meant it as an affront, the officer
   you sent me pinioned?

Rudolph. A minimum return
   for many similar favors. He's your man;
   you may have him back. He's of the stuff you like
   in councillors and statesmen—two parts crawling
   and three parts venom.

Franz Joseph. Still, without him, sir,
   I should have fared but badly. You'd have got
   just half my empire. That, if I may presume,
   should be your first lesson in government. When you're
   crowned king, leave scruples at the chancel door

with the holy water. If you keep them by you
they'll trip you up.

Rudolph. I'm not here for instruction.
Moreover the demands I made before
are altered now.

Franz Joseph. Suppose we speak in private.
  [*Taafe and Koinoff go out.*]
Looking out over the conflicts of the world
I have observed that winners make demands,
losers take what they get. You've made a play
for Hungary, and lost. You have in tow
the little Vetsera, and no doubt for you
that constitutes victory. But you may keep her
only at my pleasure. You have little reason
to raise your voice, more than a cockerel has
for his first mezzo crowing.

Rudolph. If you look
from the outer window, you'll see men ranked four deep
around the palace. No one goes out or in
without permission.
  [*Franz Joseph pauses, then goes to the window.*]

Franz Joseph. Quite unusual. Tell me,
is there some celebration?

Rudolph. These are our men.

Franz Joseph. You have no force in Vienna.

Rudolph. Try to leave.
Order your carriage. Call a servant. Ring.
You'll get no answer.

Franz Joseph. Count Taafe!
  [*John of Tuscany comes to the door.*]

John. Count Taafe is my prisoner, Your Majesty,
 but if you wish him—
  [*Taafe enters.*]

Franz Joseph. Then whose prisoner am I?

Rudolph. Shall we avoid the word? My terms are simple.
 Shall I state them to you?

Franz Joseph. You run great jeopardy
 for a trollop and a farm!

Rudolph. I'm not a novice
 in such scurrility. I could pass it back,
 but it hardly becomes us.

Franz Joseph. You have scooped up brigands
 among the socialist witlings—such as read
 Herr Sceps, his garbage, and your own—but wait.
 Wait till this slight disorder is perceived
 by authorities in the city. Hold the Hofburg
 against regulars if you can.

Rudolph. Do you recall
 what general commands in Vienna?

Franz Joseph. More than one.

Rudolph. There's been a thundering exodus tonight
 toward Buda-Pesth. Can you have been so blind,
 with all your policy, as to lock the stable
 and leave the house doors open? It's Count Hoyos
 commands Vienna. You've offended him
 in some major way.

Franz Joseph. Where is Count Hoyos?

Rudolph. Here.
 But he's been busy. It was he gave orders
 to isolate the palace.

Taafe. Hoyos too?

Franz Joseph. This may be much more serious for you all
   than I had guessed. May I look at this rebellion
   face to face?

Rudolph. Surely.

Franz Joseph. Bring them all in.
   And our little frightened captain, bring him too.
   I've something to ask him.
     [*Rudolph nods to John, who steps out.*]

     This should make history,
   what with so much nobility in one room.
   and so little mother wit!
     [*John, Hoyos, Mary Vetsera, Sceps and Koinoff enter.*]

     The good Count Hoyos,
   Vetsera, the enchanting, the truant Archduke
   who never sees his Tuscany, Herr Sceps
   of the trenchant pen, silent in council, Rudolph,
   the heir apparent. And not among them one
   to say, when they knock at my door, let the lion sleep,
   lest he be dangerous still? I am dangerous,
   and never more so than now. If you will turn
   and take your way to your homes through the silent snow
   as silently as you came, I'll not remember
   what faces I saw here, nor once remind you
   by word or act there was snow on the streets tonight
   and you left traces in it.

Hoyos. It's a little late
   to say that nothing's happened. Some of your friends
   have questioned our activities enough
   to make a stand against us. Where they stood
   the snow is somewhat bloody.

Franz Joseph. An execution?

Hoyos. No, a clash. However, not of our seeking.
   Some companies on a street corner.

Franz Joseph. How many dead?

Hoyos. That's not known yet.

Franz Joseph. And this was done, Count Hoyos,
   on your authority?

Rudolph. No, on mine.

Franz Joseph. Even that
   might be hushed up and pardoned. I engage
   to hush and pardon it if you end it here.
   Not otherwise.

Rudolph. The victors make the terms!
   That was your word!

Franz Joseph. And you are the victors?

Rudolph. Ring!
   Call your people! I saw a servant lying
   across the threshold of your hall. It seems
   he cared more for your safety than his own
   and got his throat cut.

Franz Joseph. So the boy's dead. One more
   to be explained.

Rudolph. We explain nothing. We've taken the city and hold it.

Franz Joseph. It's not a grateful task to brush the dew
   from such a gleaming dawn, but you're misinformed
   about the forces in our capital.
   There's a reserve of more than twice your numbers,
   Count Hoyos, at the arsenal. They'll be sent

to settle this night-brawling in the streets
and cut your lines outside. You'll reign but briefly.
Count Taafe, testify to this.

Taafe.
   [*To Rudolph*]
   Your Highness,
   I have been hoping you'd withdraw your men
   before you're crushed here. It's inevitable
   if you wait longer.

Franz Joseph. Perhaps you don't quite trust
   the word of the captain here, and yet he's expert
   in all these matters. He can state exactly
   what regiments are stationed in the city
   for emergencies.

Koinoff. They're lying! They're both lying!
   There are no troops at the arsenal!

Franz Joseph. Koinoff! Koinoff!
   The weathervane should make certain of the wind
   before it whirls.

Koinoff. But that's the truth, Prince Rudolph,
   there's no guard there.

Franz Joseph. Do you remember, Taafe,
   I said there was something overlooked? Even so.
   It was Count Hoyos who had slipped my mind
   when we stripped Vienna down. And so we've lost.
   At least we've lost this hand. And I accede
   to your terms, Prince Rudolph. Much against my will
   and judgment, choose out your village farm and dangle
   your lady with you. You'll rue it, and so will I,
   but take the disease with the cure.

Rudolph. It was my plan
   to take only Hungary, leave you Austria,
   but now you've pushed your stakes across the table
   and thrown your dice and lost, I win them both,
   and keep them both.

Franz Joseph. Both? Not only a farm,
   but Hungary—and not only Hungary,
   now, but Austria, too.

Rudolph. Yes.

Franz Joseph. Come. I'm to abdicate?

Rudolph. It's necessary—in cases of this sort.

Franz Joseph. You've studied them?

Rudolph. I have.

Franz Joseph. You hold a palace,
   and one old man in his room. Outside the empire
   sleeps peacefully, but when it wakes and asks
   what has been done with the emperor, you'll have
   no ready answer.

Rudolph. Tell me then what answer
   you made when in your youth you took your crown
   from the man who wore it? What's been done before
   can be done again.

Franz Joseph. Boy, you'd be followed only
   by those who stand to gain by you! The gifts
   you give to some you must take away from others!
   Could you ride a civil war?

Rudolph. Sir, by all rules
   of immemorial Austrian intrigue you
   would have the better of me. But the earth

goes steadily round the sun, and men and customs
die out or change. Shut here in your darkened room
you've seen all Europe as one static night
inhabited by spiders that sit still
mending their webs, eating their flies, and watching
each lest another spring. But, could you see,
you have not stayed the wheeling of the stars
nor held the tide piled on one longitude
by bandaging your eyes. Were I not here,
were there no men about your palace, still
your sun went down the Simplon twenty years
before tonight. What you came offering
when you were crowned, men want no longer.

Franz Joseph. Son,
   they never wanted it.

Rudolph. If I offer now
   what a new day demands, they'll come to me,
   and the old dog's forgotten. It's no pleasure
   to say this to my father, but it seems
   that in these matters sentiment's not used.
   You taught me that.

   [*Franz Joseph turns away for a moment, then comes back.*]

Franz Joseph. It might be done. If you turned orator,
   and spread the butter thick where the logic's thin
   and acted swiftly, and somewhat brutally
   while the spell was on them, you could sew them up
   before they caught their breath. But it's not your way,
   my Rudolph. No, you'd mean it while you said it,
   and trust in righteousness to bring you through
   and they'd have you by the throat.

Rudolph. I'd mean it all.

Franz Joseph. No doubt. But when an actor plays a part

he's much more moving to the audience
if he's not taken in by what he's doing
enough to weep real tears. The trick of the onion's
more effective.

Rudolph. Sir, you may hear my creed.
There's been no king, since the half-mythical figures
of medieval times, who took for his motto:
Nothing for myself. But I shall take it.
I'm tired of having. Let me drink plain water
and eat plain food, and turn what mind I have
to an instrument of justice, clean of greed,
despising politics. The first steps we take
may seem arbitrary or tyrannous,
but when we're once entrenched we'll lighten all
oppression from above, and let the garden
grow, for it will!

Franz Joseph. Suppose I abdicate.
What is your first step, being king?

Rudolph. To remove
political restrictions.

Franz Joseph. Oh, but first, I know,
say two or three hundred men in Hungary,
say three or four hundred men in Austria,
who must die if you'd be king. Oh, yes, they **must.**
And I'm among them.

Rudolph. I'd think there were not so many.
Shall we say—imprisonment?

Franz Joseph. Oh, no—they're like
the little servant who was killed outside.
While they're alive they'll fight, and they'll have friends.
Koinoff will live, the snakes will shed their skins,

but those who can't crawl must die—that's absolute,
if you're to last ten days.

Rudolph. Very well. Let them die.

Franz Joseph. Yes, a few—you'll say—men nobody wants,
but for your real antagonists, the men
with power and will and courage, you'll respect them
and let them live, because your heart's too soft
for more than a moderate slaughter. And being alive,
and having no inhibitions of your sort,
they'll rip you up.

Rudolph. And since that must be prevented
I'll be thorough.

Franz Joseph. I beg your pardon?

Rudolph. Sir,
interpret it as you please. I shall be thorough.

Sceps. This is a strange beginning, Rudolph!

John. Yes,
but logical. There's no escape from it.

Mary. Rudi—it's not the way—

Rudolph. It's the road we've taken
and can't retrace—

Sceps. Yet we'll have much the look
of the French guillotine that came, my lord,
to set men free!

Hoyos. When men make revolutions
they put their enemies to death or die.
That's beyond argument.

Rudolph. Little as we like it
some few must die.

Sceps. I don't go with you in it!
   Moreover, in matters serious as this
   you owe it to us all to ask our word
   before you make decisions!

Rudolph. I shall ask
   your word, later on, but at the moment this
   is a military action. One strong hand
   must guide it.

Sceps. If you begin, Prince Rudolph,
   with these wholesale proscriptions, my tongue and pen
   are useless to you. I'm no facile journalist.
   What I believe I'll write and publish. These
   are murderous tactics, unnecessary to
   the establishment of authority.

Rudolph. You'll no longer
   cooperate with us?

Sceps. No.

Rudolph. Why, in that case
   you'll publish nothing till we give you leave.

Sceps. You'll establish censorship? You?

Rudolph. Until it's clear
   who governs—till we're quite past being shaken
   we dare brook no opposition.

Sceps. Dare not! Dare not!

Rudolph. You heard my order!
   This is no moment for a descent of doves
   and apocalyptic revelations! Take
   your place among us or leave!
     [*Sceps is silent.*]

Franz Joseph. Your reign begins
    to shake off dreams, and may in time emerge
    as the age of iron. We agree on my demise.
    And what will you do next?

Rudolph. With Your Majesty's pardon
    our time grows short, and we have much to do.
    I can give you no more answers.

Franz Joseph. To put it plainly
    you wish to see this remnant of a monarch
    encased behind stone walls?

Rudolph. Of necessity.
    And further speech is useless. In this hour
    I'm responsible to myself alone.

Franz Joseph. It's best
    when you're in company to make pretense
    that there's a God, and you're responsible
    to Him on high. But there, I take your time.
    If I might put one question more I'll swear
    to eternal silence.

Rudolph. What is it?

Franz Joseph. When you've killed
    these seven hundred men, and they've been ushered
    solemnly under ground, what disposition's
    planned for their property? Will it be given
    to friends of yours?

Rudolph. Sir, not to my enemies.

Franz Joseph. Why, fairly answered.
    Count Taafe, stand erect. We've had the watching
    of many gallant gentlemen who passed
    this doorway for the last time. Our admiration

went with those few who took it in a stride
and laughed as they went out. I say goodnight,
adding, with the fine old piety of kings,
a hope that we meet in heaven.

Rudolph. Goodnight.

Taafe. Goodnight.

Hoyos. Shall I call a guard?

Rudolph. Yes. Take the emperor
and Taafe in your keeping. As for Koinoff
have him shot when convenient.

Koinoff. Your Majesty!

Rudolph. I want no such allegiance! Wipe him out,
and let his death come first! Let it stand as omen
over what follows!

Franz Joseph. In your place I'd keep him,
but that's a minor matter. Before I go
may I congratulate your cabinet
on the accession of an emperor
who'll give my reign, in retrospect, the air
of a golden age, in which the headsman's axe
fell as light punctuation.

John. Why do you say so?

Franz Joseph. When you grind my friends
for fertilizer, and plant your friends in their dust
I know your history.
    [*Franz Joseph and Taafe step toward the door.*]
    Now may I ask
one final favor?

Rudolph. Yes.

Franz Joseph. When the good Count Hoyos
finds me a cell, will he see that this cell's furnished
with pen and ink and paper, paper enough
to hold seven hundred names? It just so happens
that I, of all men living, can tell best
the names of my fast friends. For a legacy
I'll leave the list to you.

Rudolph. Leave it if you like.
I'll not trust it.

Franz Joseph. It will be full and accurate. One name
will be omitted, that of Count Taafe here,
because there are, say, ten or a dozen matters
he can inform you of, unfinished business
that carries over. What you may do with him
or with his information, when you have it,
that of course rests with you. Will you mind, Count Taafe,
if we leave you delegate among the living
from the kingdoms of the dead?

Taafe. At Your Majesty's service.

Rudolph. And for your information let me state
that no unfinished business carries over
from your régime to mine. I want no links
that tie us in with your machinery
for the exploitation of underlings. No doubt
you leave ten thousand questions at loose ends,
matters of foreign correspondence, matters
of internal discipline, taxes, legislation
to stop fresh gaps in the walls where liberty
begins to wear through stone. But all these questions
will go unanswered till we get to them
and answer them our own way. Our way's not yours,
has no relation to it.

Franz Joseph. You could trust him.
   I am myself too dangerous a chattel
   to keep about, but Taafe knows as much
   as I, and will serve you quite as well.

Rudolph. Have you failed
   to hear me? What in God's name is Taafe to you
   that you should plead for him?

Franz Joseph. Lad, nothing, nothing.
   I don't ask this for Taafe, but for you!

Rudolph. And I don't want him, won't have him at any price—
   want none of your retinue, nor plans nor fragments
   left over from your ruins!

Franz Joseph.
   [*Almost to himself*]
   It may be wise.
   It may be the way to win them. Yet at first
   you'll go so far astray. Well, let it go,
   Taafe comes with me.

Rudolph. Why this is kind of you.
   I thank you both.

Franz Joseph. You'll think I delay for a purpose,
   but one more word. A revolution's won
   or lost on its first morning, all depending
   on how your people take it, and your people
   depend on the press entirely. Before one word
   sifts out on your revolution, the journalists
   of both the capitals must be informed
   firmly of what to print. A censorship's
   inevitable. Herr Sceps is an indication
   of what you must expect.

Rudolph. Must I say again
    that nothing you have ever said or done
    is necessary as a precedent
    to what we have to do? You came to enslave!
    We come to set men free!

Hoyos. But if you're worried
    about the censorship, we thought of that.
    The papers have been silenced. That was my job,
    and I saw to it first.

Franz Joseph. You've seen to it! I see.
    You have two hands; with one you set men free,
    with one you shut them up. That's as it should be.
    That's as it always is.

Rudolph. Does your catechism
    draw to a close, or will you indulge us further
    with reminiscences of triumphs over
    the people you have ruled?

Franz Joseph. You have left one weakness,
    though only one. The Princess Stephanie
    is still your wife. If you should break with her
    you will get tardy recognition from
    the powers of Europe; your support at home
    will be confused. Temper your blood a while;
    postpone your union with Vetsera, or
    your kingship's mortally wounded.

Rudolph. I'm aware
    of your feeling on that question. We'd not be here
    tonight if the tempering of my blood had lain
    in your imperial hands.
    [*He turns to Mary.*]

Franz Joseph. You turn for solace
  to a rather doubtful bosom—I know this lady
  better than you—

Rudolph. Damn you, will you bring this maundering to an end?
  why all this kindly interest in me? Why,
  to poison what I'm to do, with your last breath
  infect us with your leprosy! Take them out!
  Let it end! I've listened too long!
  [*He turns his back and walks away. A pause. Taafe steps toward the
    door. Koinoff, a dagger in his hand, leaps across the room to-
    ward Rudolph.*]

Franz Joseph. Rudolph! Rudolph!
  [*He throws himself between Koinoff and Rudolph and is hurled to the
    floor. Hoyos and the Archduke John pinion Koinoff's arms
    and his knife falls. Rudolph bends over Franz Joseph, helping
    him as he gets to his feet slowly.*]

Koinoff.
  [*To Franz Joseph*]
  Why did you stop me? Do you want to die?

Franz Joseph. You mistake me, sir!
  Was I too quick for you? It's not for nothing
  I've learned to watch men's eyes! These weathercocks
  blow east and west.

Rudolph. Why do you risk your life
  to save mine?

Franz Joseph. Why, because you've forty years
  of life in you, and I have ten or twelve—
  and we're alike. I shall have no other son,
  but you may breed a dozen Habsburgs yet
  to send the name on.

Rudolph. Sir, have you joined my rebellion
  against yourself?

Franz Joseph. Why, lad, I've won! I've won!
  What I want most is to leave a king behind me
  such as I see you are!

Rudolph. You wanted this?
  You played for it?

Franz Joseph. How often what we've wanted
  comes to us in the night, a little early,
  too unexpected, and we put it by,
  and it never comes again. I take my way
  quite happily into what darkness you prescribe,
  my son, knowing now I leave behind a king
  after my heart, a better than myself,
  but a king, and a Habsburg king! He will chew on iron
  who tries to eat you, now that your salad days
  are over. When you speak you speak the words
  of Wittelsbachs and fools, but when you act
  then you're my son, and the long quarrel in your blood
  between the Empress and myself, the quarrel
  that lay in your conceiving, it's now ended,
  and I shall win, by dying.

Rudolph. I shall not **rule**
  as you have.

Franz Joseph. You'll try reforms, and then you'll learn
  that all reforms are counters in the game
  of government, played to get what you want;
  a trick of management. I tried it too,
  and found it useful. We have said goodnight—
  the guard is ready, you have things in hand,
  and I'm sorry to have kept you. Before you sleep
  look in that little black book on your desk—
  and read three words of it. I think you'll find
  it's worth your time.

  [*The prisoners are taken out, Koinoff between Hoyos and John. Mary
  and Rudolph are left together.*]

Rudolph. I am the thing I hate!
    Among us all we've made of me the thing
    I shall hate most till I die. The thing I do,
    caught on this bayonet of time, and driven,
    repeats in word for word and death for death,
    his coronation.

Mary. Once I heard you say
    a king might be a man, but a man with power
    to make men free.

Rudolph. I've come to this point in anger,
    but standing here, looking out on what's behind
    and what's before, I see in one blinding light
    that he who thinks of justice cannot reach
    or hold power over men, that he who thinks
    of power, must whip his justice and his mercy
    close to heel. My anger brought me here
    and ruthlessness will hold me where I am
    and those who are my friends are gainers by it
    but nothing's changed. I knew this as a child
    knows what's in books, as words, and I believed
    that by some ardent miracle of the mind
    I'd give my own mind wings. But what was anger
    I must now keep, and make a code, and live by,
    or be torn down.

Mary. One moment since you said it,
    let the garden grow.

Rudolph. I said it. But in this light,
    this blinding light that beats on you and me
    now as we stand here, robbing those who have
    of what they robbed from others, tell me what rule,
    what guide, what standards, human or divine,
    can possibly direct a man or king

toward justice? Is it just that men shall keep
what they already have? It was not gained justly.
The titles to possession all run back
to brigandage and murder. What men own
is theirs because they have it, remains theirs
while they can keep it. There's no other proof
of any man's deserving. I set up
my title now on murder, as my father
set his up long ago. And I take over
an old concern, maintained by fraud and force
for traffic in corruption. The rest is perfume.
A government's business is to guard the trough
for those whose feet are in it.

Mary. How can you know this?

Rudolph. I have been taken up on a crest of time
and shown the kingdoms of the world, those past,
those present, those to come, and one and all,
ruled in whatever fashion, king or franchise,
dictatorship or bureaucrats, they're run
by an inner ring, for profit. It's bleak doctrine,
it's what the old men told us in our youth,
but it's savagely true.—I know it true for me,
for when I entered this room, and knew I owned it
and knew I'd touched Franz Joseph's power, then virtue
went out of me to him; I was not the same,
and any man who sits here in his place
will be as he was, as I am.

> [*He sits at the table, placing his hand on the notebook. Mary comes
> forward and lays her hand over his.*]

Let the man live.
Let the old man live.

Mary. Don't read it.

Rudolph. No. I won't read it. I won't need it now.
    I know what I have to do.

Mary. Not for that reason.
    You'd know the writing.

Rudolph. Yes?

Mary. Because it's mine.

Rudolph. What's written in it?

Mary. It's a diary,
    Of where we went, and what we did, at first,
    when I first knew you.

Rudolph. How does it come here, Mary?

Mary. I was a little fool, and I had seen you
    somewhere at a ball—and worshipped you—
    as they all worship you, perhaps, not thinking,
    just whispering to each other in the night
    about the Crown Prince Rudolph. Then one day
    the Baronin von Neustadt took me aside to say
    she could arrange a meeting. All she asked
    was that I keep a record of my day,
    and where we went—

Rudolph. These are reports to him?

Mary. Yes.

Rudolph. This is how you came to know me?

Mary. Yes.
    Only at first—

Rudolph. I think I might forgive
    anything else you'd done, but to think of you
    along with Koinoff! Did you know Koinoff?

Mary. No.
  I warned you when I knew. Oh, Rudolph, please,
  it's nothing. There's nothing here you couldn't see
  if you wish to read them. And when I loved you, then
  I sent no more. You can believe it, truly,
  knowing how much I love you.

Rudolph. I do believe you.
  And I have loved you, but it is like Koinoff.
  These Koinoffs. They're the woman in your arms.
  They're the love she brings you. They're your love for her.
  You hear them in the music, taste them in
  the drink. It seeps and rains and drizzles Koinoffs.
  I think I must have loved you more than I knew.
  More than I knew.
      [*Hoyos and John re-enter.*]
  There was little enough left walking on this earth
  to hold a man from spitting! That's gone now!
  This was to be my lover and my queen,
  and he sent her to me, to sleep with me and tell!
  Even that was his! Let him keep it! Let him have his earth
  where men must crawl and women must crawl beneath them
  and all their words are lies! I'm sick of it,
  sick, and sick to my death!—Hoyos, the guard
  that's round the palace—send them all home to bed.
  Our revolution's over.

Hoyos. Yours may be,
  not mine. I have no wish to send myself
  the last six feet downstairs.

John. Walk out if you like,
  but I'm not through.

Rudolph. Take it. You're next in line.
  Take Austria and welcome.

John. Will you let us die
   like so many bitch's pups?

Rudolph. Why, who are we
   that we shouldn't die? Have we more reason to live
   than our seven hundred? But you won't die, you'll fix it
   or get away.

Hoyos. Is this definite?

Rudolph. Quite definite and final. But you'll live.
   And Koinoff, he'll live, too. It's an ill wind
   that brings nobody salvage. Make your arrangements,
   Hoyos, and cross the border. It's snowing still,
   and the blood we shed's been covered. The little groom
   that fell on my father's threshold, see that he's
   removed, so folks won't stumble when they enter
   and raise an outcry. I think you said the shooting's
   good at Mayerling. I shall try it. If
   you want me, look for me there.
      [*To Mary*]
      You've managed nicely
   to take my last faith from me.
      [*He turns away.*]

Mary. Am I to stay?

Rudolph. You'd better go with Hoyos. Take care of her
   for my sake, Hoyos. Look that she's safe away.
      [*He starts out the door.*]
   The devil take these dead men. I shall see
   his eyes forever.

Mary. Rudolph!
      [*Rudolph goes out.*]

CURTAIN

THE MASQUE OF KINGS

ACT THREE

ACT III

Scene: *Rudolph's apartment in the shooting lodge at Mayerling. The room is plainly furnished, containing little more than a writing table, a gun-rack and a number of chairs. There is a fireplace at the rear, also a door to the bedroom; the entrance to the hall is at the right. At the left two curtained windows. It is dawn of the next day, just beginning to lighten toward sunrise. Three shots are heard in the distance, at varying intervals, then two more, as if a covey of birds had been flushed. There is a tap at the hall door, a pause, and* Loschek *enters. He pauses, looking at the open bedroom door.*

Loschek.

[*Softly*]

Your Highness.

[*Rudolph comes out in a dressing gown, a packet of letters in his hand.*]

You wished me to call you at dawn, Your Highness.

Rudolph. Yes. It's dawn already?

Loschek. Nearly six.

Rudolph. Is Hoyos about?

Loschek. I think he's shooting in the lower copse with the others. They went out at five.

Rudolph. Yes. I heard them banging. There's nothing like fire-arms to amuse a soldier. I've been writing letters, Loschek.

Loschek. Yes, Your Highness.

Rudolph. I have addressed them in my own tangled chirography, but you've had experience with it, and I trust them to you.

Loschek. Yes, Highness.

[*He takes the letters.*]

Rudolph. Also I think your face is my earliest memory, Loschek, except perhaps for my mother's. You'll say your face is nothing much to remember, I know—

Loschek. Yes, Your Highness—

Rudolph. But the point is you've never failed me in any commission—nor in anything whatever—except for brief periods when you restricted my allowance of spiritous liquors—

Loschek. Oh, sir—

Rudolph. Thereby lengthening my life toward some highly dubious conclusion. Which conclusion, if it should be sudden, I have anticipated by penning certain laborious notes to my friends. You will keep them for me, and you will keep them where nobody will find them unless—and until. You understand me?

Loschek. Too well, Your Highness.

Rudolph. Oh, but there's nothing immediate, nothing in the least immediate. Only the news has reached me that we all die sometime. Azrael, the angel of death, came to me in the night and told me I bore a resemblance to my father. I felt a feather fall from his wing, and where it touched my temple the hair was gray this morning. As they say in the Old Testament, Selah.— When we know that we're to die what's the difference whether we're dead or not, Loschek?

Loschek. The greatest difference in the world, my lord.

Rudolph. And yet no difference at all.—In fact, I don't know yet what future my dear father plans for me, if any. I await his pleasure. Nobody knows what may go on at the back of the old man's mind. Hence the premonitions. Let me see Count Hoyos when he's finished with the partridges.

Loschek. Yes, Highness.

> [*He goes out. There are a few scattering shots from the copse and Rudolph goes to a window. Mary Vetsera opens the rear*

door and enters in a nightgown. She pauses a moment, then
speaks softly.]

Mary. Rudi.

Rudolph. Yes.

Mary. I was half awake, and reached for you with my arm,
   but you were gone; then suddenly I felt
   such deadly terror—I'd have died of it
   if I hadn't found you.

Rudolph. Or gone back to sleep
   and waked to ask for breakfast.

Mary. Rudi, please
   don't mock me—my blood's cold with it—as if
   the author of the experiment put out
   a hand and took the sun—and from then on
   it would be dark and cold. It was a dream.
   One can't tell dreams.

Rudolph. You tell them very well—
   you do everything well—perfect, finished,
   adept, accomplished—that's the woman of it;
   God knows where they learn.

Mary. Is it dawn on the windows?

Rudolph. Yes.

Mary. The sun's not gone then. But it's cold
   as if it would never be warm.

Rudolph. Go back to bed.
   I'll have them light a fire.

Mary. Whose lover were you—
   last night when you loved me?

Rudolph. I can pay.
   [*He holds out his hand with coins in it.*]
No doubt you'll recognize the sum. It's usual
here in Vienna.

Mary. Is this the wage they set
   for prostitutes?

Rudolph. You recognize it?

Mary. No,
   but I've heard, I think.

Rudolph. I've heard men say it was little
   for a woman's soul in the night. It seems her soul's
   worth more then than by day. For scrutinize it
   under broad daylight and it's plainly dirt
   like the rest of us. Take the money.

Mary. You want to hurt me?

Rudolph. These little hurts! They're fiction, like your souls,
   and they wash out like rain. With a new dress
   they're half-healed—add half a dram of starlight,
   three kisses and a ring, and they're gone clean,
   better not spoken of.

Mary. What have I done?

Rudolph. Women are realists, my dearest dear,
   loving the sun like flowers, but if one sun
   goes headlong down the sky, with Phaethon,
   they weep a little under dewy lids
   and wait for the next sun's rising. I've gone down
   and you will weep your most becomingly
   and swear it's the end, the last, and so it is
   until the next sunrise.

Mary. Why should you hurt me?
    Is it because you hate the whole earth so much
    you want to hate me too?

Rudolph. If you'll go stop
    three tradesmen on the street, and ask the three
    what it is they live by, they'll reply at once
    bread, meat and drink, and they'll be certain of it;
    victuals and drink, like the rhyme in Mother Goose
    makes up their diet; nothing will be said
    of faith in things unseen, or following
    the gleam, just bread and meat and a can of wine
    to wash it down. But if you know them well
    behind the fish-eyes and the bellies, if
    you know them better than they do, each one
    burns candles at some altar of his mind
    in secret; secret often from himself
    each is a priest to some dim mystery
    by which he lives. Strip him of that, and bread
    and meat and wine won't nourish him. Fish-eyed,
    pot-bellied, standing over counters, still
    without his chuckle-headed hidden faith
    he dies and goes to dust. The faith I had
    was baseless as a palace of the winds
    anchored in cloud, a faith that I had found
    a use for kings, a faith that with skill and wisdom
    and infinite tolerance, infinite patience, I,
    the heir of all the Habsburgs, might strike out
    a new coinage of freedom, cut new dies for the mind
    and lift men by their bootstraps till they walked
    the upper air. This is the faith of fools,
    but I had it, and I lost it. One by one
    the holds I counted on to take us up
    turned out to be the ancient clanking irons
    that bind men to the rock. Till one by one

I could trust no one—could not trust myself,
and stretched out blindly at the end to rest
on a love I had—a woman's love—not much
to ask when your world comes down about your ears
after your faith. And then I saw it there,
a little, dirty, calculating love,
smelling of stale champagne and cigarettes
and girls'-school lushing. Fit to go to bed with,
and offer coins for.

Mary. I know it. I said it once.
And now you see me as I see myself,
a baggage, the sort that might have sold you flowers
or cleaned your rooms. Once when we walked in line
out of the school, thirty girls in line, you rode
with your princess, down the Prater—and we looked
and gasped and worshipped. That's when I saw you first,
among these females in the egg, adoring
their king of men. I loved you after that,
even when I had a nasty small affair
with the officer, that, too, was in your world,
and I was almost proud. I know it's silly
to be young, to be love-sick, to make a portrait-shrine
of someone far-off, above you; but to have
the sudden offer of a meeting with him
if only you'll bring word of where he goes,
and then to find that he's incongruously
in love with you, as you with him, to know
that you're a little fool, no more, no more,
and one of the great masters of the world,
the highest, wisest, godliest, looks down
and loves this empty face of yours—oh, Rudi,
I could have wished you better than to love
where there was nothing! Then I took my soul
between my hands, and said, if this is his

it must be worthy of him; watched your ways
and listened when you spoke, and loved, and listened
till I knew better than you knew yourself
what your dreams were; yes, till it sometimes seemed
that something nobler grew here in my breast
than the heart of a gypsy's daughter. Words came to me
to say what I had never thought nor said,
and pride came, and reserve. But these are yours,
not mine, for I was moulded in the womb
after a slighter pattern. Made for dancing
or for light loves. And now you look on me
and see it. What was yours you take away
and what you leave of me will dance again
because that's all it knows, but not be happy
because it loved you once.

Rudolph. Why were you here
  last night?

Mary. Was it wrong? I've nothing that's my own.
  I followed you. I came because you came,
  not even thinking. Why did you let me in
  if I wasn't wanted?—But it was wrong. I know;
  I come between you and your father. Once
  I'm gone he'll take you back. Rudi, I swear
  I didn't think of it.

Rudolph. Think of this then, my dear;
  my date's run out; I'm no more king of men
  than Loschek. I've a pocket-full of silver,
  and certain braid on my coat, and a name I hate,
  and a strong inclination toward the dark
  like a cur dying. It's a woman's place
  to fix her to some bastard that goes up
  and set her heel on faces that go down
  as mine is going. All the rest is words,

the weeping interim, the sweet despair
before you dance again.

Mary. I'll go if it helps you.
I'll try never to see you.

Rudolph. Try? Oh, child,
look in your heart. Your hands still cling to me,
but if you're a woman, if you're human, while
you cling, your mind's alive with circling wings
searching this way and that—one man who smiled,
one man who asked you boldly for a night,
ten men who came a-wooing—of them all
which of them all shall make his bed with me
when Rudolph's gone? The treacherous, savage mind
knows betters than our words. And I know this
because my mind's more savage than your own,
filthy, desperate, faithless, hopeless of faith
in men or women or myself.

Mary. Is there no way
I could still see you, any creeping way,
so low the emperor would never know
that I was there? If I could be your dog,
even your dog—

Rudolph. You're shivering. It's cold here.
We must have a fire.
   [*He lights the fire in the grate.*]

Mary. I read a story once
about how all men vanished from the earth
after some pestilence, and a race of dogs
grew up where men are. Their religion was
that there had once been gods who walked upright,
built fires, and knew all things, and gave commands
and still lived, but invisible. I think

when I have lost you I'll remember you
as the dogs remembered man.

Rudolph. For the fires I build?

Mary. No. One must have a god. Was I faithless, Rudi?
Why did I speak when you'd have had an empire,
and warn you not to take it?

Rudolph. Because you knew
you'd lose me if I were emperor.

Mary. Would I have lost you?

Rudolph. Yes.

Mary. Yes, I would. And that was selfish, too.
Either way I must lose you. Very well.
I lose you either way.—What will you do?
Where will you go?
   [*Rudolph is silent.*]
   You'll be crown prince again.
Go back to your father.

Rudolph. Yes.—It's all one now
which way I go.

Mary. Yes. Surely.
   You'll be forgiven if you give me up,
but with me you're a beggar, as I am.
You were too chivalrous to say it out,
but that's the way it's left us.

Rudolph. As for you
the world's young yet. If you should never see me,
isn't it true, another love comes by
and whistles at your window, and it's spring,
and the great wound you thought would never heal
leaves not a scar in time—? oh, a few months

or years and all the paths that led to grief
are stopped with green-briar, overgrown and lost,
past finding when we hunt for them.

Mary. Why, yes,
oh, yes. I shall not like the thing I'll be
when that has happened.

Rudolph. When it's happened, then
we think no more about it.

Mary. Yes, but now
I'd rather be a statue to my love,
a statue in a forest, lost and unseen,
cold, too, and white, and hardly once remembered,
but changeless just the same.—Oh, but I'll go!
When feet are made for dancing they must dance
unless the heart stops.

    [*A couple of random shots are heard from the woods.*]

Rudolph. Hearts are durable;
they wear out all the rest. You're still trembling.
Come near the fire.

Mary. No, I'll go back to bed.
I think I'm tired.

Rudolph. Forgive me?

Mary. As a dog
forgives his god, see, I forgive you wholly,
and worship what you do. Only forgive me
if I should never change.

    [*She kisses him.*]

Rudolph. Yes. Rest well.

Mary. I'm happier now, and I'll rest.
> [*She goes into the bedroom and closes the door. There is a tap at the hall entrance and Loschek looks in.*]

Loschek. Count Hoyos, Highness.

Rudolph. Let him in.
> [*Loschek withdraws and Hoyos enters.*]

Hoyos. Greetings, Your Highness.

Rudolph. It seems
you never sleep.

Hoyos. I haven't your inducements.
I hear you sent for me, but I was coming
with a bit of news. A coach just topped the rise
bearing the royal arms. It looks to me
as if you had early visitors.

Rudolph. You saw it?

Hoyos. On the other side of the gates. He should be here
by this time.

Rudolph. It's the Emperor.

Hoyos. No doubt.
It struck me you'd do well to wash your face
and hide your woman.

Rudolph. How do you stand with him?

Hoyos. Well, as I said, he put us out like lightning,
gave us our pardons with the back of his hand
and combed his whiskers. I was out of favor—
I'm still out, that's all.
> [*A single muffled shot is heard.*]

Rudolph. Why is he coming?

Hoyos. Oh, just to get you back. Put in a word
for your humble servant.

Rudolph. I will. That's what I sent
to tell you now.

Hoyos. You'll kiss and make up?

Rudolph. Why not?
Between the black wolf's jaw and the lamb's hind-quarters
I'd rather play the wolf.

Hoyos. That's sensible.

Rudolph. I was born half wolf, half sheep, God pity me;
one tears the other.

Hoyos. If it's that way with you
make your terms, man.

Rudolph. Terms? When wolf eats lamb
that's terms—and peace. Wait for me.
  [*He goes into the bedroom. Hoyos walks to the fire. After a moment
     Rudolph comes out with a small revolver in his hand.*]

Hoyos.

Hoyos. Yes?
  [*Rudolph shows the revolver. Hoyos goes into the bedroom. Rudolph
     sits unsteadily. Hoyos returns.*]

When did it happen?

Rudolph. This moment. She was here.

Hoyos. I must tell the emperor.

Rudolph. No! Tell no one! Their damned kites
will take her from me!

Hoyos. What will you do?

Rudolph. I don't know yet.
  Keep them away.—She's dead?

Hoyos. She died instantly.

Rudolph. I can't believe it. Hoyos, she was here,
  before you came.

Hoyos. I must tell some story. Quick,
  what is it?

Rudolph. Keep them out. Let them leave me alone.
  She wanted to be changeless. I heard the shot
  and thought it was the hunters. Tell the king
  the Crown Prince Rudolph came to Mayerling
  to seek seclusion. Hold them off with that
  and tell them nothing.

Hoyos. Lad, I know it's awkward
  to see a pretty woman that you've known
  with a bullet through her head. But don't let that
  mislead you. It's an embarrassment the less
  once you've run dry of tears. Suppose we're quiet
  till I can smuggle her quietly under-ground.
  Then if she's travelling in Italy
  or Turkestan and never does come back
  at least she's gone.

Rudolph. Damn you, what do you mean?

Hoyos. Only that we say nothing. You yourself
  suggested it.

Rudolph. Then do as I suggest,
  and leave me with her.
    [*Hoyos goes toward the door. As he approaches it there is a knock and
      he opens to Loschek.*]

Hoyos. Who is it?

Loschek. The Empress, sir.
She asks me to tell Rudolph that she begs
on her knees to see him.

Rudolph. Why should she beg of me?
She may come if she likes.

[*Loschek steps back, and after a moment the Empress Elizabeth
enters.*]

Elizabeth. What is it, Rudolph?
What's in your face?

[*She goes across and kneels beside him.*]

Rudolph. The black jaw's at the flock,
that's all.

Elizabeth. What is it, Hoyos?

Hoyos. We've both been rebels;
maybe we're sorry for it.

Elizabeth. It's something more.
As if you'd watched a pageant cross the night
with horror at the end.

Rudolph. Oh, mother, mother,
so many, many times, I needed you
when I was a child, but you were never there,
and now we're strangers.

Elizabeth. They kept me from you!

Rudolph. Yes.
And now we're strangers. What you'd have me do—
all that was worth the saving in me, that
was you, and I've betrayed it.

Elizabeth. But all we've lost,
all the lost years, we'll have them now. Look, Rudolph,

your father's with me. This night long he wept,
a pitiful, shrunken king, because his child
despises what he does. Come back to him.
I've been against him always, as you have,
but we've grown old together, and his son
means more to him than kingdoms. He's forgotten
whatever it was that happened, forgives it, pardons
all that took part, asks nothing, only to have
his man-child back again.

Rudolph. Yes—as before.

Elizabeth. Will you see him?

Rudolph. Yes.

Elizabeth. He's waiting, Hoyos.

Hoyos. Yes, madam.
   [*He goes out.*]

Elizabeth. You haven't slept.

Rudolph. No.

Elizabeth. It's quite useless, Rudolph,
   to fight against what we are. It's broken me.
   It will break you too.

Rudolph. You have gone over to them.

Elizabeth. Only to help you.
   [*There is a short pause, then Franz Joseph enters. They rise.*]

Franz Joseph. Lest you should think I deal
   in crocodile promises, Rudolph, I have here
   three long state papers, drawn in a sleepless night,
   and signed and sealed. One is full pardon for
   your friends and you, another's a commission
   left blank that you may choose what place you'll take

in the Austrian government—and this, the third,
will place you on the throne of Hungary
three years from now, even if I live so long
and you're not there before. I offer these
as humbly as I can. Lose you I cannot.
Let you go I cannot. If I've been
too politic, too stern, forgive me, Rudolph,
I went to a bitter school.

Rudolph. What else?

Franz Joseph. I hold
to one condition only. The Vetsera's
a light, designing woman, bought and sold,
loving by instinct where she lies, but quick
in trade, like the trader's daughter that she is,
where a kiss will mean advantage. She's no queen
for you. The mirror on her wall has kept
as full a record as her heart of those
she'll reach her arms out for.

Rudolph. I told her that,
and have her answer that she'll never change
after this morning.

Franz Joseph. You believed her?

Rudolph. Yes.

Elizabeth. There should be something regal in a queen,
Rudolph; she's small and cheap.

Rudolph. But she'll not change,
after this morning. A statue in a wood
runs more in the rain, yields more to the frost, than she
in this last mood.

Elizabeth. Is she here?

Rudolph. Yes.

Elizabeth. May I see her?

Rudolph. Mary! Mary Vetsera!
    [*There is a pause.*]

Elizabeth. She's asleep?

Rudolph. Yes.

Elizabeth. Shall I wake her?

Rudolph. Wake her if you can.

Elizabeth. What is it, Rudolph?
    [*She looks at Rudolph's face, then crosses to the bedroom and enters.*
    Returning, she leans heavily against the door-jamb, her eyes
    fixed first on Rudolph then on the Emperor.]

Franz Joseph. I understand.
    [*He walks to the door, looks through it briefly, then turns to Eliza-*
    beth.]

  It will be necessary to conceal
  our visit here. Hoyos will bring us word
  of what has happened to the Hofburg.—You
  will come with us.

Rudolph. I shall stay here to make
  the necessary arrangements.

Franz Joseph. It must not be known.
  that you were with her. Nothing in the world
  could clear your name of scandal, or suppress
  the story if you remain.

Rudolph. She's quite immune
  to scandal now, and I shall not greatly mind
  what's said of me.

Elizabeth. Rudolph, Rudolph, it's your name,
  your name before the people! Say you loved her,
  still nothing you do or say can hurt her now,
  and you have a life to live!

Rudolph. If I go back
  this morning, and leave her lying in this room
  alone, then hour by hour you'll win me from her,
  and in the end it will be my hand that guides
  all Europe down to hell. I know myself
  and what you'll want of me, and what I am,
  and my black destination. But I've learned
  from the little peddler's daughter, the Vetsera,
  how to keep faith with the little faith I have
  quite beyond time or change.

Franz Joseph. For the love of God!

Rudolph. You have no God, nor I! When a man lies down
  to sleep, he sleeps!

Elizabeth. My child, my child, don't think it!
  It tears my heart!

Rudolph. My mother was a rebel,
  and she used all her beauty and her brain
  to check the darkening evil of a house
  that thrives and grows by evil. She's here now,
  an angel still, but fallen, holding out
  to me the bloody symbols of the trade
  by which we've lived too long. And if I live
  I'll wear them, as she wears them, till my mind's
  a charnel house, and men remember me
  as the breath of pestilence! I had thought, indeed,
  of going back with you, but I'll die young
  and pleasanter to remember.

Franz Joseph. Must we believe
    that the first prince of Europe, in his pride
    of mind and hope, will die for love—the love
    of a basket-woman's child?

Rudolph. Sir, in your sanity
    you'll never glimpse what thin partitions part
    our life and death, to a dweller on the threshold.
    This prince is only a walking apparatus
    for oxidation, a web of water, spun
    to last one morning. A morning more or less
    will hardly count.
        [*A burst of gun-fire is heard from the wood.*]

Elizabeth. Let me have this, at least,
    out of my sacrifice, that the son I bore
    to be a Habsburg king, will be a king;
    let me have this! Whatever else I had
    when I was young is gone now, melts beneath
    a finger's touch, like the tapestries they lift
    into air from a Pharaoh's tomb. When I have walked
    the Hofburg rooms, this alone was real, that you
    were Rudolph, and my son, and would be king
    though the very walls dissolve, and I dare not speak
    to those I pass lest there be no one there
    but my imagining.

Rudolph. We are all ghosts, we three,
    walking the halls of Europe in a dream
    that's ended, a long masquerade of kings
    that crossed the stage and stumbled into dark
    before we came. We are the shadows cast
    by medieval conquerors, a rout
    of devil-faces, thrown up long ago
    by the powers beneath erupting, but long dead
    and gone to slag. Now the earth boils up again

and the new men and nations rise in fire
to fall in rock, and there shall be new kings,
not you or I, for we're all past and buried,
but a new batch of devil-faces, ikons
made of men's hope of liberty, all worshipped
as bringers of the light, but conquerors,
like those we follow. I leave the world to them,
and they'll possess it like so many skulls
grinning on piles of bones. To the young men
of Europe I leave the eternal sweet delight
of heaping up their bones in these same piles
over which their rulers grin. To the old and dying
I leave their dying kingdoms to be plowed
by the new sowers of death—fools like myself
who rush themselves to power to set men free
and hold themselves in power by killing men,
as time was, as time will be, time out of mind
unto this last, forever. We are all ghosts,
we three, but from today I shall not haunt
the Hofburg halls, Habsburg or Wittelsbach,
wolf, sheep or shadow. So saying, light of heart,
I lie with the Vetsera.

> [*He makes one of his stiff little bows, steps into the bedroom, with-*
> *drawing from royalty, and closes the door. Elizabeth runs to*
> *it.*]

Elizabeth. Rudolph, Rudolph—
you cannot, cannot—Rudolph, open to me,
your mother!

> [*There is a shot within the room.*]

Franz Joseph. We have no son.

> [*Hoyos enters.*]

Elizabeth. Hoyos, here—quick,
It's Rudolph—

Hoyos. What has he done?

Elizabeth. Break down the door!
He went in—he may be only hurt!
Hoyos—Hoyos!

Hoyos. I shall need help with this.

Elizabeth. Help him, Franz.

Franz Joseph. Help him? We have no son.
Leave this pawing of doors. He was too much
a prince not to die if he wished. And he is dead.

Elizabeth. You wished him dead!

Franz Joseph. I loved him. I must think now
how to go on without him.

Elizabeth. How to go on!
What could we go toward now?

Franz Joseph. Toward that same darkness
he prophesies, perhaps—Oh, Rudolph, my son,
would I had died for you. Would I had died.—
This must be covered up. We have not been seen here.
Hoyos will bring us word to the palace. Get
the girl in the earth tonight. An accident—
a hunting accident—

    [*There is faint gun-fire in the distance.*]

    Toward that same darkness
he prophesies—

CURTAIN